WITHDRAWN

P9-DWQ-396

The Food Lover's Guide to Chocolate and Vanilla

OTHER BOOKS BY SHARON TYLER HERBST

The Food Lover's Guide to Meat and Potatoes

The Food Lover's Tiptionary

The New Food Lover's Companion

*Wine Lover's Companion (*with Ron Herbst*)*

The Joy of Cookies

Breads

Cooking Smart

Simply Sensational Desserts

The Food Lover's Guide to

Chocolate and Vanilla

Sharon Tyler Herbst

William Morrow and Company, Inc.

New York

Copyright © 1996 by Sharon Tyler Herbst

All rights reserved. No part of this book may be reproduced or utilized
in any form or by any means, electronic or mechanical, including photo-
copying, recording, or by any information storage or retrieval system,
without permission in writing from the Publisher. Inquiries should be
addressed to Permissions Department, William Morrow and Company,
Inc., 1350 Avenue of the Americas, New York, N.Y. 10019.

It is the policy of William Morrow and Company, Inc., and its imprints
and affiliates, recognizing the importance of preserving what has been
written, to print the books we publish on acid-free paper, and we
exert our best efforts to that end.

Library of Congress Cataloging-in-Publication Data

Herbst, Sharon Tyler.
The food lover's guide to chocolate and vanilla / Sharon Tyler Herbst.
p.   cm.
Includes index.
ISBN 0-688-13770-9
1. Cookery (Chocolate) 2. Cookery (Vanilla)   I. Title.
TX767.C5H44 1996   95-47558
641.6'374—dc20   CIP

Printed in the United States of America

First Edition

1 2 3 4 5 6 7 8 9 10

BOOK DESIGN BY RICHARD ORIOLO

Acknowledgments

A basic truth known to every author is that a book would simply not become a book without the intricate support system composed of family, friends and colleagues. And so, with tremendous gratitude and affection, I offer a heartfelt thank-you and verbal hug to . . .

Ron Herbst—my husband, hero and best friend—for being my business and creative consultant, spirit lifter, computer expert, trusted taster and, when there was little time for anything but writing and testing, for cooking dinner or taking me out.

Harriet Bell, my exceptional editor, who enthusiastically enlightens, guides and believes in me, and whose sense of humor *always* makes me laugh.

Gail Kinn and Ann Bramson, the wonderful editors who made sure this book received the perfect finishing touches.

Sonia Greenbaum, copy editor, who so skillfully minded my *p*'s and *q*'s and even found a better way to express some of my ideas.

All the behind-the-scenes people at Morrow who so diligently worked on the design, layout, printing and everything else it took to bring this book together.

Fred Hill, my literary agent, for his insight, wisdom and urbane wit, and for taking my "Irish" with his calm, cool manner.

The dear friends who have been willing and enthusiastic tasters, sampling dishes both wonderful and not-so-wonderful-yet, making suggestions and generously sharing ideas: Sally and Stan Bernstein, Bobbi and Ted Campagna, Ruth and Phil Hicks, Lee and Susan Janvrin, Glenn and Laura Miwa, and Dan and Kimberley Young.

And, as always, my dear parents, Kay and Wayne Tyler, and sister, Tia Tyler Leslie, for their unending encouragement, love and support (and their gentle exhortations not to work so hard).

Contents

Introduction

For the Love of Chocolate and Vanilla

There's no doubt about it—the two most asked for flavors in America are, you guessed it, chocolate and vanilla. Each stands in a distinctive class by itself for being both exciting to work with and extraordinarily versatile. It's true that whereas vanilla once reigned as America's favorite flavor, chocolate has now taken the lead. But there's no arguing that vanilla is by far the more versatile of the two flavors. It is a fact that more people "crave" chocolate than they do vanilla, but then chocolate is a much more aggressive flavor and by its very nature commands a passionate response. I've always thought of chocolate and vanilla as the "yin and yang" of the culinary world—chocolate being the bolder, more masculine force, with vanilla as its sweet, exotically feminine counterpart. Separately, both chocolate and vanilla evoke emotional responses ranging from passion to comfort. Together, they create a celebration for the senses.

The following recipes range from casual to sophisticated, from easy to elaborate and from slightly naughty to wickedly decadent. There are fruity enticements like Chocolate Razzmatazz

Shortcake and Chocolate-Cherry Clafouti; quick tempters, including Almost-Instant Vanilla Silk and S'more Pie; updated classics such as Fudged Banana Cream Pie and Black Bottom Crème Brûlée, and drop-dead decadent desserts like Chocolate Seduction Mousse Cake and Tunnel of Fudge Cheesecake. Make no mistake—there's nary a nonfat, artificially sweetened dish in the lot. All of these desserts are *seriously* indulgent. Studies have shown that the great majority of people would rather have one bite of a luscious dessert than a full-size portion of something low calorie and nonfat, with its intrinsically synthetic flavor and odd texture. I agree unequivocally. A truly rewarding dessert should be a grand finale, not a lackluster compromise.

In the end, there should *never* be any compromise when it comes to chocolate and vanilla. Separately, these two flavors are hallmarks of natural wonder. In concert, chocolate and vanilla are enticingly irresistible and exquisitely delicious—in short, the stuff from which the sweetest dreams are made.

Ingredients

Besides chocolate and vanilla, the ingredients most often used in this book are butter, eggs, flour, sugar. Here's what I used to test the recipes:

■ *Butter:* I always use unsalted butter for its pure flavor. If you substitute regular (salted) butter, slightly decrease the salt called for in the recipe. To quickly soften butter, remove foil wrapping, put butter on a plate in a microwave oven and cook at MEDIUM-LOW (30 percent) power for 30 to 60 seconds.

■ *Eggs:* The term "egg(s)" refers to *large grade-AA eggs. See pages 18, 27, 66, 75, and 91 for more information on eggs.*

■ *Flour:* I used either all-purpose flour or cake flour in these recipes. The *all-purpose flour* is unbleached and presifted. Most of the recipes don't call for sifted flour—simply stir it well, then spoon it lightly into the measuring cup, leveling off with the dull edge of a knife. *Cake flour* is made from a fine-textured, high-starch soft wheat that produces tender baked goods. If you don't have cake flour, substitute 1 cup of all-purpose flour less 2 tablespoons for each cup of cake flour.

■ *Sugar:* Three types of sugar are used in the following recipes—granulated, brown and confectioners'. Superfine sugar is a fine, almost powdery granulated sugar that's perfect for meringues. If you don't have any on hand, process regular granulated sugar in a food processor fitted with the metal blade for about one minute.

■ *Sugar substitutions:* 1 cup regular granulated sugar = 1 cup superfine sugar, 1 cup firmly packed brown sugar or 1³/₄ cups confectioners' sugar.

Chocolate

*It has been shown as proof positive that carefully prepared chocolate
is as healthful a food as it is pleasant; that it is nourishing and easily digested;
that it does not cause the same harmful effects to feminine beauty which are
blamed on coffee, but is on the contrary a remedy for them. . . .*

—Jean-Anthelme Brillat-Savarin

In his remarkable tome *The Physiology of Taste, or Meditations on Transcendental Gastronomy,* Frenchman Brillat-Savarin, an avowed chocolate lover, devotes several pages to its universal allure. The above quotation reminded me in particular of a basic truth every food professional knows in his or her bones—there are few new realities in the culinary world. This witty, distinguished lawyer-gastronome was writing about women and chocolate 170 years ago, and today there's a best-selling book on the subject of why women need chocolate. It is, I confess, a book I didn't buy, for I have always been one of those individuals for whom chocolate is more than a casual acquaintance but is, instead, a passionate, sensuous connection to all my hedonistic yearnings.

The word "chocolate" comes from the Aztec *xocolatl* (later transliterated to *chocolatl*), meaning "bitter water." Indeed, the unsweetened drink the Aztecs made of spices, vanilla and pounded cacao beans (from a tree the Aztecs held divine) was said to be extremely bitter. The taste obviously didn't deter Aztec emperor Montezuma, who is said to have consumed up to fifty golden goblets of the potion daily. True, Montezuma's seemingly excessive consumption was undoubtedly linked to the fact that he believed the heady concoction to be an aphrodisiac, but then it's always important for royalty to keep up appearances.

How did the rest of the world discover the Aztecs' secret? Pundits tell us it's only logical that Columbus returned to Spain with cocoa (or cacao) beans among his New World treasure trove, but if so, they were overlooked in the excitement. In fact, chocolate wasn't duly noted until the sixteenth century, when Spanish explorer Hernando Cortés returned from conquering Montezuma's empire with, among other treasures, some highly prized cocoa beans and cuttings for replanting.

Although the Spanish were impressed with chocolate's purported restorative powers and health-giving properties, they were not fond of its bitter taste. It was soon discovered, however, that this strange chocolate potable was deliciously seductive when sweetened with sugar.

From Spain, chocolate was introduced to Europeans, who embraced it with an enthusiasm bordering on passion. In the eighteenth century, America began manufacturing chocolate—its popularity spread in part, undoubtedly, because the esteemed statesman-connoisseur Thomas Jefferson touted its healthful benefits. Finally, in the mid-nineteenth century, a British confectioner developed a technique for creating extravagantly smooth eating chocolate. And that, as they say, was definitely the start of something *big*.

But let's get back to chocolate's reputation for stimulating effects. Was this all in the Aztecs' imagination? Was Casanova fooling himself to value chocolate above champagne as a tool for seduction? Perhaps not entirely. Chocolate contains theobromine, a bitter, colorless alkaloid with a mild stimulant effect (similar to caffeine) that, among other things, dilates blood vessels and stimulates heart muscles. Chocolate also naturally contains phenylethylamine, an antidepressant that acts as a mood elevator to create a feeling of well-being and elation very much like the heady sensation that accompanies the feeling of being in love. Looks like the Aztecs knew a good thing when they tasted it.

In truth, few other foods elicit such passion as the rich, dark manna we know as chocolate. Unapologetically and in the sweetest sense, chocolate has seduced and conquered the world. Quite simply, it is for those who love it—wickedly delicious, irresistibly voluptuous, enticingly luxurious and, in the end, the ultimate indulgence.

How Chocolate Is Made

Chocolate comes from the tropical cocoa bean, *Theobroma* (Greek for "food of the gods") *cacao*. The bulging cacao pods, which grow directly from the tree's trunk and major limbs, are cut open to reveal an average of thirty almondlike seeds or beans. After the beans are removed from the pods, they're fermented, cleaned, dried and briefly roasted for flavor enhancement. The shells of the now-dried beans then crack and fall off, leaving the nibs—the "meat" of the cocoa bean. The nibs (which contain an average of 54 percent cocoa butter, a natural vegetable fat) are ground to extract some of the cocoa butter, leaving a thick, dark brown paste called "chocolate liquor," the basis of all forms of chocolate.

Next, the chocolate liquor receives an initial refining. If additional cocoa butter is extracted, the solid result is ground and sifted to become unsweetened cocoa powder. If the chocolate liquor is to be made into eating chocolate, it's further processed by a technique called "conching." During this process, huge mechanical rollers slowly blend and "knead" the heated chocolate liquor, ridding it of residual moisture and volatile acids. The conching continues for 12 to 72 hours, depending on the type and quality of the final chocolate. During conching, other ingredients (such as additional cocoa butter, sugar and milk powder) are often added. The last step for most eating chocolate is tempering, a heating-and-cooling process that produces its final lustrous sheen and melting texture.

Chocolate-Related Terms

Bloom: Pale gray streaks or blotches on the surface of chocolate. These are actually cocoa butter crystals that have formed because the chocolate was stored in too warm or too damp an environment. Bloom has no effect on a chocolate's flavor.

Cacao: The name of the tropical evergreen tree that's cultivated for its fruit (large pods containing beans) from which chocolate, cocoa powder and cocoa butter are obtained. The term "cacao" also used to refer to the plant's raw product.

Chocolate liquor: A thick, dark brown paste made from the cocoa bean's ground nibs. This paste is the basis and essence of all other forms of chocolate; the more chocolate liquor a product contains, the richer it is. When chocolate liquor hardens, it's called "unsweetened chocolate." And, no, it has no alcoholic content.

Cocoa butter: The natural, cream-colored vegetable fat extracted from cocoa beans during the process of making chocolate and cocoa powder. Cocoa butter contributes to the flavor, texture, sheen and meltability of chocolate.

Nibs: The "meat" of the cocoa beans, which are separated from the shells during processing (see "How Chocolate Is Made," page 7) and contain an average of 54 percent cocoa butter.

Conching: A chocolate-manufacturing process by which "huge" mechanical rollers slowly blend and knead heated chocolate liquor, eliminating residual moisture and volatile acids and thereby mellowing the flavor and smoothing the texture.

Lecithin: A fatty substance obtained from legumes, used in the manufacture of chocolate as a moisturizer and emulsifier. Lecithin sometimes replaces some of the cocoa butter in chocolate.

Seizing: When a minute amount of liquid or steam comes in contact with melted chocolate, it seizes, or begins to clump and harden. Seizing can also occur when the heat used to melt chocolate is above 120°F. For how to correct seizing, see "Tips on Working with Chocolate," pages 11–13.

Tempering: A melting-and-cooling technique for stabilizing the cocoa butter crystals in chocolate to make it more malleable and glossy. Commercially available chocolate is tempered but goes out of temper when chocolate is melted or improperly stored. When that happens, the surface can form the dull gray streaks or blotches called "bloom." Tempering chocolate isn't necessary for most recipes, but is often done when making candy or decorations.

The *classic tempering method* is to melt chocolate until it reaches a temperature of 115°F. Two thirds of the melted chocolate is then spread on a marble slab and worked back and forth with a metal spatula until it becomes thick and cools to a temperature of about 80°F. This thickened chocolate is then transferred back into the remaining third of the melted chocolate and reheated to about 89°F for semisweet chocolate, and about 85°F for milk or white chocolate. The *quick tempering method* is to melt two thirds of the chocolate to 115°F, then add the remaining third of the chocolate, finely chopped, to the melted mixture, stirring until the mixture reaches 89°F and is smooth.

Types of Chocolate

Chocolate and cocoa products are classified according to percentages of key ingredients (like chocolate liquor, milk solids, etc.) that conform with the FDA's (Food and Drug Administration's) Standards of Identity. Each manufacturer has developed its own special formula, but in general the following descriptions characterize the various commercially available chocolate products. The words in SMALL CAPITALS are defined in the section on "Chocolate-Related Terms" (page 8).

Unsweetened chocolate (also called *bitter* or *baking chocolate*) must contain 50 to 58 percent COCOA BUTTER and is hardened CHOCOLATE LIQUOR.

Semisweet and bittersweet chocolate must, by weight, be at least 35 percent CHOCOLATE LIQUOR. They also contain sugar, added COCOA BUTTER, LECITHIN (an emulsifier) and vanilla or other flavorings. These two chocolates can vary slightly in sweetness but are generally interchangeable. "Semisweet chocolate" is primarily an American term, whereas Europeans more commonly label their version "bittersweet chocolate." Semisweet chocolate is the most popular choice for cooking and is available in chips (regular, giant and miniature) and bar form.

Sweet chocolate is dark chocolate that contains at least 15 percent CHOCOLATE LIQUOR; it also has flavorings and more sugar than semisweet chocolate.

Cocoa powder is CHOCOLATE LIQUOR (with some of the fat extracted) that has been dried and powdered. This *unsweetened* powder contains 10 to 22 percent COCOA BUTTER. Dutch-process cocoa powder (also called European style) has been treated with an alkali, which helps neutralize cocoa's natural acidity and make it more soluble. The flavor is slightly more mellow, the color darker. When substituting Dutch-process cocoa powder for regular cocoa powder, omit the baking soda (which acts as an alkalizer) in the recipe.

Liquid chocolate (also called *premelted chocolate*) is a mixture of cocoa powder and vegetable oil. It doesn't have the same flavor or texture of melted unsweetened chocolate primarily because it doesn't contain as much COCOA BUTTER.

Milk chocolate must contain at least 12 percent milk solids and a minimum of 10 percent CHOCOLATE LIQUOR. It also contains sugar, COCOA BUTTER and vanilla or other flavorings. Because of the heat sensitivity of the milk protein, this chocolate is not recommended as a dark-chocolate substitute.

Couverture is a specially formulated professional-quality dark coating chocolate that is extremely glossy. It contains a minimum of 32 percent COCOA BUTTER. Couverture is generally only available in specialty candymaking shops or a baker's supply house.

White chocolate isn't truly chocolate because it doesn't contain CHOCOLATE LIQUOR. It is typically a mixture of sugar, COCOA BUTTER, milk solids, LECITHIN and vanilla. Carefully read the label of any such product—if it doesn't contain cocoa butter, it's not white chocolate. Because white chocolate has a tendency to scorch and clump when overheated, it must be melted over very low heat. It should not be substituted for other chocolates.

Confectionary coating (also called *compound* or *summer coating*) is not considered chocolate, but is used in the same manner for dipping candies. Confectionary coating is a blend of sugar, milk solids, hardened vegetable fat and flavorings. It should never be substituted for chocolate.

Note: Beware of products labeled "artificial chocolate" or "chocolate-flavored." Just as the label states, these aren't the real thing, a fact that's evident in both flavor and texture.

Chocolate Substitutions

When making chocolate substitutions, mix the butter with the fat called for in the recipe and the cocoa powder and sugaw with the dry ingredients.

Unsweetened chocolate, 1 ounce: 3 tablespoons unsweetened cocoa powder plus 1 tablespoon butter or shortening

Premelted unsweetened chocolate, 1-ounce envelope: 3 tablespoons cocoa powder plus 1 tablespoon vegetable oil

Semisweet chocolate, 1 ounce: $1/2$ ounce unsweetened chocolate plus 1 tablespoon granulated sugar; or 1 tablespoon cocoa powder, plus 1 rounded tablespoon granulated sugar, plus 2 teaspoons butter or shortening

Sweet chocolate, 4-ounce bar: $1/4$ cup unsweetened cocoa powder, plus $1/3$ cup granulated sugar, plus 3 tablespoons butter or shortening

Tips on Working with Chocolate

Storing Chocolate

• Chocolate should be stored, tightly wrapped, in a cool (60° to 70°F), dry place. Under ideal conditions, dark chocolate can be stored for years. However, the

milk solids in both milk chocolate and white chocolate shorten their storage life to about 9 months. When chocolate is stored at warm temperatures, it develops a pale gray "bloom" (surface streaks and blotches), caused when the cocoa butter rises to the surface. Chocolate that's been stored in damp or cold conditions can form tiny gray sugar crystals on the surface. Though unsightly, such discolorations don't typically affect the flavor.

Melting Chocolate

• Spray the container you use to melt the chocolate with nonstick vegetable spray and the melted chocolate will slip right out.

• Chocolate will melt more quickly if you cut it into relatively small pieces. Chocolate chips melt faster than squares. Various chocolates have different consistencies when melted: Unsweetened chocolate becomes runny; semisweet, sweet and white chocolate hold their shape until stirred.

• Melt chocolate slowly—it scorches easily, which completely ruins its flavor. White chocolate is particularly sensitive to scorching and so should therefore be handled with extra care.

• The microwave oven is one of the best ways to melt chocolate. Put the chocolate in a microwave-safe container and heat at MEDIUM (*50 percent power*). Four ounces of chocolate will take about 3 minutes in a 650- to 700-watt oven; the timing will vary depending on the oven and the type and amount of chocolate. One-ounce, paper-wrapped squares of chocolate can easily be microwaved right in the paper to save on cleanup—1 square takes $1\frac{1}{2}$ to 2 minutes, 2 squares about 3 minutes, and 3 squares about 4 minutes.

• Chocolate can also be melted in the top of a double boiler over simmering water. Remove the top of the double boiler from the heat when the chocolate is a little more than halfway melted and stir until chocolate is completely smooth.

• To melt chocolate for decorating, put finely chopped chocolate or chocolate chips in a small, heavy-duty plastic bag (if the bag's not heavy duty, it could melt). Set the unsealed bag upright in a small bowl and microwave at MEDIUM (*50 percent power*) until almost melted; let stand 5 minutes until completely melted. *Or* seal the bag and set in a bowl of very hot water until chocolate is melted (make sure that no water gets into the chocolate). Thoroughly dry the bag with a paper towel before snipping a tiny hole in a corner of the bag. Pipe a decorative design directly onto a dessert. The chocolate can also be piped onto a sheet of waxed paper, refrigerated until set, then transferred onto the dessert.

• Though chocolate can be melted with liquid (at least $\frac{1}{4}$ cup of liquid per 6 ounces of chocolate), a single drop of moisture in melted chocolate will cause it to seize (clump and harden). Seizing can also occur when chocolate is melted at a heat above 120°F. *To correct seized chocolate,* stir a small amount (no more than 1 tablespoon per 6 ounces of chocolate) of clarified butter, cocoa butter or vegetable oil into the chocolate. Slowly remelt the mixture and stir until smooth. It should be noted that the added fat may affect the texture of the final product.

• Cool melted chocolate to room temperature before adding it to cookie doughs or cake batters. Adding hot melted chocolate could cause a textural change in the baked product.

Grating Chocolate

• Grated chocolate can be used to decorate or garnish all kinds of desserts from cakes to ice cream.

• Room-temperature chocolate is easier to grate than chocolate that's too warm or too cold.

• To grate chocolate by hand, start with a large, thick piece—it's easier to handle. Place a box grater over a piece of waxed paper. Hold one end of the chocolate in a piece of paper towel to prevent the heat of your hands from melting it. Firmly rub chocolate over coarse side of grater. *Or* use a Mouli rotary grater for fast and easy results.

• Chocolate can be grated in a food processor in several ways. Using either the thin slicing blade or the grating disk, gently press chocolate into blade with the plunger. *Or* break chocolate into small chunks and chop with the metal blade, using ON/OFF pulses.

• Run a vegetable peeler across a chilled bar of chocolate to create chocolate flakes.

• Refrigerate grated chocolate until ready to use.

Devil's Delight Chiffon Cake

My friend Yei Miwa makes wonderful chiffon cakes. They're light and moist, and my inspiration for creating the yin to her yang: a tall and devilishly dark and chocolaty chiffon. Don't bother to brew a pot of coffee—simply dissolve 1 tablespoon instant espresso powder (or 1½ tablespoons regular instant coffee) in 2 tablespoons hot water, then add enough room-temperature water to equal ¾ cup. If you use Dutch-process cocoa powder, omit the baking soda.

Serves 10 to 12

2 cups sifted cake flour

⅔ cup unsweetened nonalkaline cocoa powder, such as Hershey's

2 cups sugar

1 tablespoon baking powder

½ teaspoon baking soda

½ cup canola or other vegetable oil

6 egg yolks, room temperature

¾ cup strong coffee, room temperature

1 tablespoon pure vanilla extract

8 egg whites, room temperature

1 teaspoon salt

1 teaspoon cream of tartar

About 1 tablespoon confectioners' sugar

Preheat oven to 325°F. Set aside an ungreased 10-inch tube pan.

In a large bowl, whisk together flour, cocoa powder, 1⅓ cups of the sugar, baking powder and baking soda. Make a well in the center of the dry ingredients. Add oil, egg yolks, coffee and vanilla; beat until smooth.

In a large mixing bowl, beat egg whites, salt and cream of tartar until they form soft peaks. Beating constantly at medium speed, gradually add remaining ⅔ cup sugar, 2 tablespoons at a time, beating until the whites form glossy, stiff peaks. Stir ¼ of the whites into the chocolate mixture to loosen the batter. Gently fold in remaining whites, a third at a time, using a large rubber spatula and a minimum of strokes to retain body and diminish deflation of the egg whites. Don't overwork the mixture—it's okay to leave a few streaks in the batter.

Gently spoon batter into pan; smooth surface. Bake 1 hour and 10 minutes, or until surface just springs back when lightly pressed with your fingertip. Immediately invert cake in pan onto a cake rack or over a narrow-necked bottle. Cool completely in pan. Removing the cake from the pan before it's thoroughly cool will cause it to fall.

Run a thin knife around pan between cake and side of pan; repeat with center tube. Turn cake out onto cake plate, rapping pan bottom, if necessary, to release cake. Dust with confectioners' sugar. Serve with vanilla-scented whipped cream or vanilla ice cream.

To dream of cake foretells advancement for the laborer and enhancement for the industrious. . . . Layer cake denotes satisfaction. . . . A fluffy rich icing on a cake predicts gaiety.

—Ned Ballantyne and Stella Coeli
Your Horoscope and Dreams

Black Magic Mousse

Of all the cooking classes I've taught, those on chocolate are the most popular. And this relatively easy recipe is, hands down, always a class favorite. One caveat: This intensely flavored fusion of chocolate and coffee is for dedicated chocophiles only—it's definitely not for the faint-hearted. If you're alcohol sensitive, substitute ¼ cup cream and an extra teaspoon of coffee powder for the Kahlúa. For ultimate decadence, make Chocolate Seduction Mousse Cake (page 19), which combines this mousse with chocolate chiffon cake.

Serves 8 to 10

2 tablespoons instant coffee powder

¼ cup Kahlúa or other coffee-flavored liqueur

12 ounces bittersweet or semisweet chocolate, finely chopped

*5 eggs, separated, room temperature

2 teaspoons pure vanilla extract

¼ teaspoon salt

½ teaspoon cream of tartar

¼ cup sugar

2 cups whipping cream, whipped to firm-peak stage

Additional whipped cream for garnish (optional)

*See "Do You Trust Your Eggs?," page 27

In a 2-cup glass measure, combine coffee powder and Kahlúa. Microwave on HIGH for 30 seconds; stir to dissolve. Add chocolate; microwave on HIGH for 1 to 1½ minutes. Stir until chocolate is melted and mixture is smooth. *Or* combine instant coffee, Kahlúa and chocolate in the top of a double boiler. Stir over simmering water until chocolate is halfway melted. Remove top of double boiler from bottom pan; stir until chocolate is melted and mixture is smooth.

For either method, whisk egg yolks, one at a time, into chocolate mixture, blending well after each addition. Turn mixture into a large bowl; stir in vanilla.

Cool to room temperature, stirring occasionally; don't let mixture set.

In a large mixing bowl, beat egg whites with salt and cream of tartar at high speed to soft-peak stage. Beating constantly, gradually add sugar, 2 tablespoons at a time. Continue beating until sugar is dissolved and whites are glossy and firm; set aside. Stir ⅓ of the whipped cream into chocolate mixture to loosen; gently fold in remaining whipped cream. Fold in egg whites, a third at a time. Spoon mousse into a 2-quart glass bowl or 8 to 10 stemmed glasses. Refrigerate for at least 2 hours. Garnish with dollops of whipped cream, if desired.

Eggs: Cracking Up May Lead to Separation Anxiety

■ When cracking an egg, you're less likely to break the yolk if you crack it on a blunt surface like the rounded edge of a bowl.

■ To avoid unpleasant bits of eggshell in your batter, don't crack an egg directly into a mixture, particularly one that's being beaten with an electric mixer. Instead, break eggs one by one into a small bowl or cup before adding them to the main mixture. This technique will also save the day if there's a bad egg.

■ Though it's easier to separate eggs when they're cold, egg whites will reach their fullest volume when beaten at room temperature. The best thing to do is separate the eggs when they're cold and let them stand at room temperature for about 20 minutes so they can warm up a little.

■ Because there could be minute bacteria on an eggshell's surface, it's not a good idea to separate eggs by passing the yolk back and forth from one half of the shell to the other.

■ An inexpensive egg separator makes separating eggs a breeze. Or try gently cracking them into a funnel over a bowl— the yolk stays in the funnel while the white passes through. Or simply cup your hand and crack the egg into it—the white falls through your fingers while the yolk stays nestled in your palm. Needless to say, wash your hands well with soap and water afterward.

Chocolate Seduction Mousse Cake

A veritable dessert spectacular worthy of the most special occasions. True, it's labor-intensive, but some events, not to mention people, are simply worth the extra effort.

Serves 10 to 12

Devil's Delight Chiffon Cake (page 14)
Black Magic Mousse (page 16)
2 cups whipping cream
2 tablespoons confectioners' sugar
2 teaspoons pure vanilla extract
2–3 tablespoons grated semisweet
  chocolate

Prepare cake according to directions. Prepare mousse, increasing chocolate to 14 ounces.

Using a serrated knife, gently cut a 1-inch layer from top of cake; set aside. Cut around cake 1 inch from outer edge and 1 inch from center hole. Carefully remove cake from center with your fingers or a spoon, leaving a cavity with 1-inch walls and a 1-inch base. Freeze removed cake pieces for future use. Spoon mousse into cake cavity until even with top of cake. Replace reserved cake slice on top. Cover and refrigerate for at least 6 hours or overnight.

Beat cream until it forms soft mounds. Add sugar and vanilla; beat until cream forms stiff peaks. Frost cake with whipped cream; garnish top with grated chocolate. Refrigerate until ready to serve.

Chocolate-Cherry Clafouti

Clafouti (pronounced *klah-foo-TEE*) is a simple country dessert that originated in France's Limousin area. Some clafoutis are cakelike, while others resemble custard—this one's closer to the latter. The chocolate is my touch, but quite natural, I think, considering chocolate's affinity for cherries. Although sour cherries are traditionally used in clafouti, fresh ones are hard to find in most areas, so I use sweet varieties—Bings, Lamberts or Tartarians—which, to my palate, make a better match with the chocolate. Although canned cherries can be used for this dessert, extra care must be taken to drain them *thoroughly*—then shake them in the strainer and drain them again. Otherwise, excess liquid can make the clafouti too wet. A definite plus with using canned, pitted cherries is that you can put this dessert together in about 5 minutes. And some of the cherry liquid can be substituted for an equal measure of the milk. I don't recommend using frozen cherries for this recipe.

Serves 6 to 8

*4 cups pitted fresh sweet cherries
    (about 2 pounds)*
*1/2 cup miniature semisweet chocolate
    chips*
2 cups milk
1/2 cup all-purpose flour
*1/3 cup unsifted, unsweetened cocoa
    powder*
1/2 cup granulated sugar
2 teaspoons pure vanilla extract
1/4 teaspoon salt
5 eggs
About 1 tablespoon confectioners' sugar
About 1 cup whipping cream (optional)

Preheat oven to 350°F. Lightly oil a 2-quart oval gratin dish or other shallow baking dish. Distribute cherries evenly over bottom of dish, then sprinkle with chocolate chips; set aside. In a blender jar, combine ½ cup of the milk, flour, cocoa powder, granulated sugar, vanilla and salt. Cover and blend at low speed, gradually increasing to high, until well blended. Stop machine and scrape down sides of blender jar. Add eggs and remaining 1½ cups milk; blend to combine. Pour batter over fruit (some cherries and chocolate chips will rise to surface). Bake 60 to 70 minutes, or until a dinner knife inserted in the center comes out *almost* clean. Cool on a rack 15 minutes before dusting with confectioners' sugar. Don't worry, it's natural for clafouti to fall a little. Serve warm, with cream if desired. Refrigerate leftovers.

Picking Perfect Cherries

■ Choose intensely colored, shiny, plump cherries that are quite firm but not hard. Stemmed cherries are a better buy, but those with stems last longer. Don't trust your eyes when buying cherries. The simple fact is that sometimes the most gorgeous specimens have practically no flavor at all. So always taste before you buy—the produce department shouldn't mind the loss of one cherry, and you won't go home with a bag of flavorless fruit.

■ Store unwashed cherries in a plastic bag in the refrigerator for up to 5 days; wash just before using.

■ Pitting cherries is the pits, but there are several ways to make it easier. For one, there's a tool called (appropriately enough) a cherry pitter, which pops out the seed without bruising the fruit. Or you can use the tip of a vegetable peeler, a pointed knife or even a paper clip (pull one end out straight and use the opposite end as a hook). Last but not least, try the inscrutable chopstick—push it in the stem end and through the cherry, and the pit will pop right out.

Chocolate

Butterfinger Bread Pudding

I created this decadent, crunchy-topped dessert for my peanut butter–loving husband, Ron, whose favorite candy bar happens to be a Butterfinger. The chocolate–peanut butter custard can be made with either 1 or 2 percent low-fat milk or whole milk. The results are equally delicious. Likewise, you can substitute reduced-fat peanut butter for the regular kind. Butterfingers have a tendency to crumble when they're chopped, but a few large chunks will add interest to the topping. This pudding is particularly good served warm—the timing should be just about right if you put it in the oven 30 to 40 minutes before you sit down to eat.

Serves 8 to 10

4 cups milk

³/₄ cup smooth peanut butter

²/₃ cup unsifted unsweetened cocoa powder

1¹/₃ cups packed light brown sugar

2 teaspoons pure vanilla extract

¹/₂ teaspoon ground cinnamon

¹/₄ teaspoon ground nutmeg

5 eggs, well beaten

1 (1-pound) loaf cinnamon-raisin bread, untrimmed, cut or torn into ¹/₂-inch chunks or cubes

2 (2.1-ounce) Butterfinger candy bars, coarsely chopped

1 cup whipping cream (optional)

Lightly oil a 9 × 13-inch baking pan; set aside. In a blender jar, combine 1 cup of the milk, peanut butter, cocoa powder, brown sugar, vanilla, cinnamon and nutmeg. Cover and process on low speed, gradually increasing to high. Stop machine and scrape down sides of blender jar. Add eggs; process until well blended. Turn into a large bowl; stir in remaining 3 cups milk. Add bread cubes, stirring well to moisten all pieces. Let stand 15 minutes, stirring 2 or 3 times during that period. Turn into prepared pan. (If desired, pudding may be covered and refrigerated for up to 2 days at this point; let sit at room temperature for 1 hour before baking.)

While bread is soaking, preheat oven to 325° F. Bake pudding, uncovered, for 30 minutes. Remove from oven; sprinkle with chopped Butterfingers. Bake 10 more minutes, or until a knife inserted in the center comes out *almost* clean. Place pudding 3 inches from preheated broiling unit and broil until bubbly and brown, about 1 minute. Serve warm, with cream if desired. Refrigerate leftovers. Single servings can be reheated in the microwave oven on high for 30 to 60 seconds, depending on the serving size.

Bread cast upon the water comes back éclairs.

—Bert Greene

Bread Pudding Pointers

■ Almost any kind of bread can be used for bread pudding—French, Italian, butter-rich brioche, egg-rich challah and flavor-enhanced loaves like cinnamon-raisin bread.

■ Whether or not you leave the crust on the bread is up to you. Crust adds texture for those who like a little "chew" in their bread pudding. On the other hand, trimming the crusts delivers a lighter pudding. Remember that not all crusts are alike: I leave the soft crust on cinnamon-raisin bread, but I trim the crisp crust off French bread. Don't throw out the crusts—use them to make bread crumbs in a food processor with a metal blade. Freeze the crumbs for future use.

■ Slightly dry bread will soak up the liquid better. To slightly dry out fresh bread, place the bread pieces in a single layer on an ungreased baking sheet. Bake at 250°F for about 20 minutes.

■ For a richer pudding, substitute half-and-half or whipping cream for all or part of the milk.

■ For a lighter and less caloric pudding, use nonfat or low–fat milk.

■ Reducing the amount of milk or adding more eggs will create a firmer pudding; adding more milk produces a pudding with a softer, more custardy texture.

■ Personalize any bread pudding by adding 1/2 to 1 cup of raisins, chopped dried fruit, toasted chopped nuts, coconut, cranberries, chopped apples . . . you get the idea.

■ For the lightest bread pudding, beat the whites separately and fold them in just before baking.

Bourbon Street Mud Pie

This bittersweet, intensely chocolate pie is definitely an adults-only dessert. If you're not a fan of bourbon, Kahlúa or any other coffee-flavored liqueur makes a delicious substitute.

Serves 8

1 cup whipping cream

¹/₄ cup bourbon

1 tablespoon instant coffee powder or granules

12 ounces semisweet chocolate, finely chopped

*4 eggs, separated, room temperature

2 teaspoons pure vanilla extract

1 recipe Chocolate Crispie Crust and Topping (page 26)

¹/₄ teaspoon cream of tartar

¹/₂ cup whipping cream, whipped and flavored with sugar and bourbon (optional)

*See "Do You Trust Your Eggs?," page 27

In a medium saucepan, stir together cream, bourbon and instant coffee. Heat over medium heat until mixture comes to a simmer (bubbles begin to appear around edges of pan). *Or* prepare in a microwave oven: Combine first 3 ingredients in a 4-cup glass measure. Microwave on high for 2¹/₂ minutes. Remove cream mixture from heat; add chocolate and let stand 2 minutes. Stir until chocolate is melted and mixture is smooth. For either method, lightly beat egg yolks. Whisking constantly, slowly drizzle yolks into chocolate mixture, blending until smooth. Stir in vanilla. Chill, stirring occasionally, until mixture is cold (do not let it set), about 30 minutes. It will cool more quickly if you transfer the mixture from the container in which it was heated to another bowl.

While filling is cooling, prepare Chocolate Crispie Crust and Topping.

Beat chilled chocolate mixture until it forms soft peaks; set aside. Beat egg whites with cream of tartar until stiff but not dry. Stir ¹/₃ of the egg whites into chocolate mixture to loosen. Fold in remaining egg whites, a third at a time. Turn mixture into prepared crust, mounding in center. Sprinkle chocolate-covered crispie topping pieces over surface of pie, starting in about 1 inch from crust so there's a visible border of filling; use the back of a spoon to lightly press crispies into surface of pie filling. Refrigerate for at least 4 hours. If desired, garnish with sweetened, bourbon-flavored whipped cream.

Pie Pan Sizes

All pie pans are not created equal. For instance, a 9-inch pie pan may range in depth from 1 to 2½ inches, which can make a difference in the final appearance of a pie. The piecrust for the Bourbon Street Mud Pie (page 24), for example, will be thicker in a 1-inch-deep pie pan than in one that's 2½ inches deep. Likewise, in a shallow pan the filling will mound higher in the center than in a deeper pan. To check the size of a pie pan, measure the diameter from the rim's inside edge; measure the depth by placing a ruler vertically on the countertop next to the pan.

Chocolate Crispie Crust and Topping

Although I created this crust for the Bourbon Street Mud Pie (page 24), it's great with any number of pie fillings, such as coconut cream and banana cream. These ingredients also create delicious, easy snack bars that will please the kid in anyone.

Makes 1 (9-inch) piecrust

3 cups Rice Krispies or other crispy rice cereal
1 cup finely chopped pecans
6 tablespoons butter, cut into 6 pieces
4 ounces semisweet chocolate, finely chopped
1/4 cup corn syrup, preferably dark

In a large bowl, combine cereal and pecans; set aside. In a medium microwave-safe bowl, combine butter, chocolate and corn syrup. Microwave on HIGH for 1 1/2 minutes. Let stand 1 minute; stir until smooth. *Or* combine butter, chocolate and corn syrup in a small saucepan. Heat over medium heat, stirring often, until chocolate has melted and mixture is smooth. For either method, drizzle chocolate mixture over cereal-nut mixture; use a rubber spatula to lightly fold ingredients together until the crispies are evenly coated with chocolate.

Sprinkle 1 cup of the mixture onto a small baking sheet or pan lined with waxed paper. Use 2 forks to separate crispies into small pieces to form topping; refrigerate. Turn remaining mixture into a lightly oiled 9-inch pie pan. With the back of a spoon, press mixture over bottom and up sides of pan; refrigerate until set, about 10 minutes.

■ **Chocolate Crispie Treats:** Prepare recipe through first paragraph (if desired, substitute 1 cup additional Rice Krispies for the nuts). Turn mixture into a lightly oiled 8- or 9-inch square pan. Use the back of a spoon to firmly compact mixture, taking care not to smash Rice Krispies. Refrigerate until firm, about 20 minutes. Cut into 16 (about 2-inch) squares, cutting 4 strips each way.

Do You Trust Your Eggs?

Although salmonella-infected eggs can be a problem in some parts of the United States (mainly in the northeastern and mid-Atlantic states), the truth is that salmonella-related food poisoning from eggs is relatively rare. Most such cases originate in commercial establishments and are caused by improper handling, such as letting raw-egg preparations stand at temperatures that invite bacterial growth. Nevertheless, if you live in an area where egg safety is in question, or if you suffer from a weakened immune system, it's best to *avoid all raw-egg preparations entirely* and to use eggs only in recipes that will be cooked to a temperature of 160°F, which will kill almost any bacteria.

Pasteurization kills salmonella and occurs when eggs are heated at 140°F for $3\frac{1}{2}$ minutes. Since egg whites coagulate between 144° and 149°F, and yolks between 149° and 158°F, any method of cooking eggs (such as poaching) in which the white is thoroughly set and the yolk has begun to thicken is sufficient to kill most salmonella.

By far the easiest solution is to use *pasteurized liquid whole eggs,* available in cartons in a market's refrigerated section. To use this product in making pancakes, batters or baked goods that call for regular (shell) eggs, substitute $\frac{1}{4}$ cup of liquid whole eggs for each large regular egg, or $\frac{1}{8}$ cup for each egg yolk. Note that pasteurized liquid whole eggs are not the same as egg substitutes, which contain about 80 percent egg whites, plus nonfat milk, tofu, vegetable oils, emulsifiers and other ingredients.

Pear-Berry Chocolate Crumble

The flavors of raspberry and chocolate add pizzazz to this old-fashioned dessert—pears napped with a decadent raspberry cream and crowned with a crispy chocolate-oat topping. In the summer, when they're at their peak, peaches make a particularly lovely substitute for the pears.

Serves 6

1¹/₂ tablespoons cornstarch

¹/₂ teaspoon freshly ground nutmeg

¹/₄ teaspoon ground cinnamon

¹/₄ teaspoon salt

1 tablespoon pure vanilla extract

¹/₂ cup seedless raspberry preserves,
*   well stirred*

3 tablespoons whipping cream

2¹/₂ pounds (about 6 medium or 4 large)
*   firm-ripe pears such as Bosc or Anjou,*
*   peeled, cored and cut into*
*   ¹/₄-inch slices*

¹/₃ cup all-purpose flour

3 tablespoons unsweetened cocoa powder

¹/₃ cup packed light brown sugar

5 tablespoons cold unsalted butter,
*   cut into 10 pieces*

¹/₃ cup old-fashioned or quick-cooking oats

Sweetened softly whipped cream or
*   vanilla ice cream (optional)*

Preheat oven to 400°F. Lightly oil an 8-inch square baking pan; set aside. In a small bowl, combine cornstarch, nutmeg, cinnamon and salt. Stir in vanilla, blending until smooth. Add raspberry preserves and 3 tablespoons cream, whisking until smooth. Layer half of the pears over the bottom of the baking pan; drizzle evenly with ¹/₂ of the raspberry mixture, spreading it over the pears with the back of a spoon. Repeat with remaining pears and raspberry mixture.

In a food processor fitted with the metal blade, combine flour, cocoa powder, sugar and butter. Process in quick ON/OFF pulses until butter chunks are the size of small peas. *Or* combine flour, cocoa powder, sugar and butter in a medium bowl and cut together with 2 knives or a pastry blender. Stir in oats; sprinkle mixture evenly over fruit. Bake for 25 minutes, or until juices begin to bubble up around edges and top is crispy. For a crisper top-ping, place baking pan under the broiler, 3 inches from heat source, for 1 to 2 minutes. Cool on a rack. Serve warm with whipped cream or vanilla ice cream; if desired.

Notes on Oats

There are several kinds of oats (commonly called oatmeal) in markets today. *Old-fashioned (rolled) oats* have been steamed, then flattened into flakes. *Quick-cooking oats* have been cut into several pieces before being steamed and flattened. *Instant oats* have been cut into very small pieces and precooked before being dried, a process that makes them unsuitable as a substitute for other types of oats in recipes. Old-fashioned oats and quick-cooking oats are usually interchangeable in recipes, whereas instant oats can turn baked goods like muffins or cookies into gooey lumps.

Macadamia Dream Bars

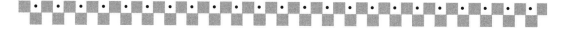

A rich fudge ribbon swirls through these chewy white chocolate bars, loaded with macadamias. You'll need a 7-ounce container of macadamias, which means there'll be a few left over. If you don't eat them while making these cookies, store them in the refrigerator, as their high fat content makes them highly susceptible to rancidity.

Makes 32 bars

Dream Bars

³/₄ cup butter, softened

1¹/₄ cups sugar

4 eggs

¹/₂ teaspoon salt

¹/₄ teaspoon ground cinnamon

2 teaspoons pure vanilla extract

1 cup all-purpose flour

2 ounces semisweet chocolate, melted and cooled

¹/₃ cup miniature semisweet chocolate chips

4 ounces white chocolate, melted and cooled

1¹/₄ cups finely chopped dry-roasted macadamia nuts, divided

Chocolate Glaze

4 ounces semisweet chocolate, coarsely chopped

3 tablespoons whipping cream

1 teaspoon pure vanilla extract

Dream Bars

Preheat oven to 350°F. Grease a 9 × 13-inch baking pan; set aside. In a large mixing bowl, beat butter and sugar until light and fluffy. Add eggs, salt, cinnamon and vanilla. Beat until thoroughly combined, scraping bowl often. Add flour; gently beat just until combined. Transfer 1 cup of the batter to a medium bowl. Stir in melted semisweet chocolate, then chocolate chips; set aside. Stir melted white chocolate and ¾ cup of the macadamias into remaining batter. Turn into prepared pan; smooth surface. Drop heaping tablespoons of the chocolate batter into the light batter in 8 or 9 randomly spaced places. Using back of tablespoon, press chocolate batter down into light batter. Use a butter knife to swirl the batters in a wide zigzag pattern to create a marbled effect; don't overdo it. Bake 20 to 25 minutes, or until a toothpick inserted in the center comes out *almost* clean. Do not overbake. Cool completely on rack.

Chocolate Glaze

In a double boiler over simmering water, melt chocolate and cream together, stirring until smooth and creamy. *Or* combine chocolate and cream in a 1-cup glass measure; microwave on HIGH for 1 minute. Let stand 1 minute; stir until smooth. With either method, stir in vanilla. Spread glaze over top of cooled cookies; sprinkle with remaining ½ cup macadamias. Chill 15 minutes to set glaze. Using a sharp pointed knife, cut into 32 bars, cutting 4 strips lengthwise and 8 strips crosswise.

And when we add the delicious perfume of vanilla to this mixture of sugar, cacao and cinnamon, we achieve the ne plus ultra *[ultimate] of perfection, to which such a concoction may be carried.*

—Jean-Anthelme Brillat-Savarin

Chocolate Tiramisù

The translation for tiramisù (pronounced *tih-ruh-mee-SOO* or *tih-ruh-MEE-soo*) is "carry (or pick) me up." The unspoken continuation must surely be "to heaven," for the to-die-for pleasure it delivers. Mascarpone, the delectable Italian cream cheese traditionally used in tiramisù, can be found in Italian markets, specialty cheese shops and some supermarkets. It is admittedly very expensive—about $11 for a 17.5-ounce tub (a generous 2 cups). However, the markedly different flavor and texture of American cream cheese make it unsuitable as a substitute. So, either pay the price of mascarpone (after all, you probably won't be making tiramisù that often) or use the following Mock Mascarpone, which comes reasonably close to the real thing. One last note: The ladyfingers sometimes found in bakeries are typically softer than the supermarket kind and will produce a lighter dessert.

Serves 12

1³/₄ cups espresso or very strong coffee
³/₄ cup plus 3 tablespoons sweet Marsala
About ³/₄ cup sugar
About 36 ladyfingers
2 cups (about 1 pound) mascarpone or Mock Mascarpone (page 33)
*6 eggs, separated, room temperature
6 ounces semisweet chocolate, melted and cooled
1 tablespoon pure vanilla extract
¹/₈ teaspoon salt
4 ounces semisweet chocolate, grated or shaved

*See "Do You Trust Your Eggs?," page 27

In a small bowl, combine coffee, ³⁄₄ cup of the Marsala and ¹⁄₃ cup of the sugar; stir to dissolve sugar. Split ladyfingers; brush both sides generously with coffee mixture. The cake should be soaked, but not fall-apart soggy. The amount of dipping liquid needed will depend on how dry the ladyfingers are. Line the bottom of a 9 × 13-inch baking pan with a single layer of soaked ladyfingers, positioning them close together; set aside.

In a large bowl, beat mascarpone and 3 tablespoons sugar until smooth. Add egg yolks and cooled melted chocolate, blending until thoroughly combined. Add vanilla and remaining 3 tablespoons Marsala, mixing to blend well; set aside. Beat egg whites and salt to soft-peak stage. Beating constantly, add ¹⁄₄ cup sugar, 1 tablespoon at a time. Beat until whites are glossy and firm. Gently fold in whites, a third at a time, into mascarpone mixture.

Spoon half the cheese mixture over ladyfingers, spreading to edges of pan; sprinkle with half the grated chocolate. Top with a second layer of ladyfingers, then remaining cheese mixture. Sprinkle remaining grated chocolate evenly over surface. Cover tightly and refrigerate overnight, or for at least 8 hours.

Mock Mascarpone

2 (8-ounce) packages cream cheese,
  softened
¹⁄₄ cup sour cream
6 tablespoons whipping cream

Beat cream cheese and sour cream until soft and smooth. Add whipping cream, 2 tablespoons at a time, beating after each addition.

Mocha-Kahlúa Tortoni

This spectacular torte is a seductive amalgam of chocolate, coffee and almond flavors. Amaretti are intensely crisp, light *almond*-macaroon cookies, found in gourmet markets and some supermarkets. Don't substitute coconut macaroons…well, you can, I suppose, but the dessert's flavor will be entirely different.

Serves 10 to 12

*3 eggs, separated

3/4 cup sugar, divided

1 1/2 tablespoons instant espresso powder or 3 tablespoons instant coffee granules

1/8 teaspoon salt

1 cup half-and-half

4 ounces semisweet chocolate, finely chopped

1/2 cup Kahlúa or other coffee-flavored liqueur, divided

2 cups whipping cream, whipped until firm

1 cup amaretti or other crisp almond-macaroon cookie crumbs

Mocha Whipped Cream (page 44)

Chocolate Leaves (page 48) (optional)

20 coffee-bean candies (optional)

*See "Do You Trust Your Eggs?," page 27

In the top of a double boiler, whisk together egg yolks, 1/2 cup of the sugar, espresso powder and salt. Gradually stir in half-and-half. Cook over simmering water, stirring constantly, until mixture thickly coats the back of a metal spoon. Remove top of double boiler from bottom pan; place on work surface. Add chocolate; stir until melted. Stir in liqueur; turn into large bowl. Cool to room temperature or refrigerate, stirring often, until cool. Speed cooling by setting bowl inside a larger bowl filled with ice water. Don't let mixture set.

Lightly oil a 9-inch springform pan; set aside. Beat egg whites at high speed to soft-peak stage. Beating constantly, add remaining 1/4 cup sugar, 2 tablespoons at a time. Beat until whites are glossy and firm. Fold egg whites, whipped cream and cookie crumbs into cooled chocolate mixture. Turn into prepared pan; smooth top. Cover with foil; freeze for 6 hours or overnight.

Run a thin knife around edge of pan; remove side of pan. Run a thin knife between the crust and bottom of pan to loosen torte. Use 2 large metal spatulas to gently transfer torte from bottom of pan to serving plate. Decorate top perimeter of torte with rosettes of Mocha Whipped Cream. Place Chocolate Leaves, pinwheel-fashion, fanning out from center of torte. Or garnish with Mocha Whipped Cream and coffee-bean candies.

I think if I were a woman I'd wear coffee as a perfume.

—John Van Druten

Peanut Brownie Torte

A fudgy brownie layer topped by a billow of peanut butter cream. There's no denying that this is a *sinful* dessert, but you can assuage your conscience somewhat by using reduced-fat peanut butter, which contains 3 grams less total fat (½ gram less *saturated* fat) per serving. A little rationalizing goes a long way!

If you're in a rush, use a 1-pound 5.2-ounce package of fudge brownie mix, preparing according to box directions and baking 20–25 minutes, or until a toothpick comes out *almost* clean.

Serves 10

Brownie Base
³/₄ cup butter
1 cup firmly packed light or dark
    brown sugar
¹/₄ teaspoon salt

4 ounces semisweet chocolate,
    finely chopped
*2 eggs
2 teaspoons pure vanilla extract
³/₄ cup all-purpose flour
¹/₂ cup chopped unsalted peanuts

Peanut Butter Layer
1 ounce semisweet chocolate,
    finely chopped
2 tablespoons whipping cream
1 (8-ounce) package cream cheese, softened
1 cup sugar
1 cup smooth peanut butter
1 tablespoon pure vanilla extract
1¹/₂ cups whipping cream, whipped to
    firm-peak stage

*See "Do You Trust Your Eggs?," page 27

Brownie Base

Preheat oven to 350°F. Grease a 9-inch springform pan; set aside. In a medium, heavy saucepan, combine butter, sugar and salt. Cook over medium heat, whisking often, until butter is melted and mixture is combined. Remove from heat. Add chocolate; stir until melted. Whisk in eggs, one at a time, beating well after each addition. Stir in vanilla, then flour, blending only until well combined. Stir in peanuts. Turn into prepared pan; smooth surface. Bake 25 minutes, or until a toothpick inserted in the center comes out almost clean. Cool completely on rack.

Peanut Butter Layer

When brownie base is cool, combine chocolate and 2 tablespoons cream in a small bowl. Heat in microwave oven on HIGH for 30 seconds. Stir until smooth; set aside to cool slightly.

In a large bowl, beat cream cheese and sugar until smooth and creamy, scraping bowl as necessary. Add peanut butter and vanilla; beat until fluffy and smooth. Fold in whipped cream, a third at a time, blending well after each addition. Spoon over brownie base; use the back of a kitchen tablespoon to create decorative swirls on surface. Drizzle cooled chocolate-cream mixture over top of torte in a lacy pattern. Cover and refrigerate at least 4 hours.

To serve, run a thin knife between pan and torte to loosen; release and remove side of pan. Use a long, narrow knife to loosen brownie base from bottom of pan. Carefully transfer torte to serving dish.

Course, we don't get meat as often as our forefathers
but we have our peanut butter and radio.

—Will Rogers

Did You Know

. . . that peanut butter was developed in 1890 and promoted as a "health food" at the 1904 St. Louis World's Fair?

. . . that about 822 peanuts go into making an 18-ounce jar of peanut butter?

Chocolate Razzmatazz Shortcake

This shortcake is decidedly different from the traditional biscuit topped with strawberries. Instead, it boasts a moist, fudgy cake layered with raspberries and cream swirled with a raspberry puree. Although to my taste the chocolate and raspberries are the perfect match, strawberries are also delicious. If using strawberries, cut them in raspberry-size chunks.

Serves 8

1³/₄ *cups all-purpose flour*

¹/₃ *cup unsweetened cocoa powder*

²/₃ *cup granulated sugar*

2¹/₂ *teaspoons baking powder*

¹/₂ *teaspoon baking soda*

¹/₂ *teaspoon salt*

¹/₂ *cup cold butter, cut into 8 pieces*

¹/₂ *cup semisweet chocolate chips*

2 eggs

¹/₂ *cup half-and-half*

3 teaspoons pure vanilla extract, divided

4 cups fresh raspberries

2 cups whipping cream

About ¹/₄ cup confectioners' sugar

Preheat oven to 400°F. Grease a 9-inch springform pan or round cake pan; set aside. In a medium bowl, combine flour, cocoa powder, sugar, baking powder, baking soda and salt. Using a pastry cutter or 2 knives, cut in butter until mixture resembles coarse crumbs. Stir in chocolate chips. In a small bowl, lightly beat eggs, half-and-half and 1 teaspoon of the vanilla. Add to flour mixture, stirring just until dry ingredients are moistened. *Or* prepare in a food processor: Place flour, cocoa powder, sugar, baking powder, baking soda, and salt in workbowl fitted with metal blade; process 15 seconds. Add butter; process in quick ON/OFF pulses until mixture resembles coarse crumbs. Add chocolate chips; pulse twice to mix. In a small bowl, lightly beat eggs, half-and-half and 1 teaspoon of the vanilla together. With machine running, add liquid mixture; process only until dry ingredients are moistened.

With either method, turn mixture into prepared pan, spreading evenly. Bake

15 to 20 minutes, or until a toothpick inserted in the center comes out clean. Cool in pan set on a rack.

In a blender or food processor fitted with the metal blade, puree 1 cup of the raspberries. Strain puree through a fine sieve to remove seeds; set aside. (Berries may be pureed and strained a day in advance.) Set aside 1 cup of the berries for garnish.

Beat cream until the consistency of thick pudding. Add remaining 2 teaspoons vanilla and confectioners' sugar to taste.

Continue beating until cream forms very firm peaks. Fold in remaining 2 cups raspberries, then gently fold in raspberry puree just so that it forms streaks—too much folding will turn the whipped cream pink.

Using a serrated knife, cut shortcake in half horizontally. Place bottom half on serving plate; top with half of berry-cream mixture, spreading evenly to edges. Place second half of shortcake on top. Repeat with remaining berried cream. Garnish with reserved 1 cup berries. Refrigerate up to 6 hours before serving.

Beautiful Berries

■ No matter what kind of berries you're buying (raspberries, strawberries, etc.), choose those that are brightly colored, fresh-smelling and plump. Avoid soft, shriveled or moldy specimens. Berries do not ripen after being picked. Strawberries should have their hulls attached. However, hulls attached to blackberries and raspberries are a sign that the berries were picked too early and will undoubtedly be tart. Always check the bottom of a berry container at the market. If the basket is see-through, look for unripe, bruised or moldy berries. If it's a cardboard basket, be sure it's not stained with berry juice, which tells you some berries are crushed, if not rotten.

■ Berries won't bruise or spoil as readily if stored in a single layer on a paper towel–lined jelly-roll pan or other large container with shallow sides. Discard any bruised or moldy berries; lightly cover remaining berries with paper towels and refrigerate for up to 3 days.

■ Wash berries just before using. Some—like strawberries—can become waterlogged, so wash quickly but gently. Refrigerated berries aren't as likely to bruise while washing as room-temperature berries.

Black Satin Sauce

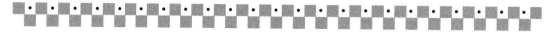

I named this rich, fudgy sauce for its lustrous sheen and the way it drapes seductively over everything from puddings to cakes to ice creams. Not only is it enticingly thick but it takes only minutes to make. If you're making it at the last minute and don't have whipping cream on hand, substitute ¾ cup milk and ⅓ cup butter. This easy-to-make sauce is perfect for gift giving.

Makes about 1¾ cups

½ cup unsweetened cocoa powder

1 cup sugar

⅛ teaspoon salt

¾ cup whipping cream

4 tablespoons butter, cut into 4 pieces

1 teaspoon pure vanilla extract

In a medium, heavy saucepan, thoroughly combine cocoa powder, sugar and salt. Slowly stir in cream, blending until smooth. Add butter; cook over medium-low heat, stirring constantly, until mixture comes to a boil. Reduce heat to low; cook, stirring constantly, for 2 minutes. Remove from heat. Cool for 15 minutes before stirring in vanilla. Serve warm or at room temperature. Sauce becomes very thick when it cools. Store, tightly covered, in refrigerator for up to 2 weeks. To reheat after refrigeration, warm in top of double boiler over simmering water. Or heat sauce in a microwave oven on HIGH for about 1 minute (stirring after 30 seconds), or until sauce reaches desired texture.

- **Raspberry-Fudge Satin:** Substitute ¼ cup Chambord (black-raspberry liqueur) for ¼ cup of the cream; add ½ cup stirred seedless raspberry preserves.

- **Mandarin-Fudge Satin:** Substitute ¼ cup Grand Marnier or orange juice for ¼ cup of the cream; add ½ cup orange marmalade.

- **Mocha Satin:** Substitute ¼ cup Kahlúa for ¼ cup of the cream; add 1 tablespoon instant coffee powder or ½ tablespoon instant espresso powder along with cocoa powder.

Chocolate Pastry Crust

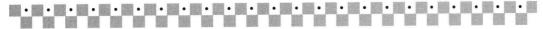

This chocolaty crust is a delicious change of pace from plain pastry. And there's no rolling out the crust with it—simply press the dough into the pan and bake.

Makes 1 (9-inch) piecrust

About 4 tablespoons unsweetened cocoa powder, divided

1 cup plus 2 tablespoons all-purpose flour

1/3 cup sugar

1/4 teaspoon salt

1/2 cup cold butter, cut into 6 pieces

1 teaspoon pure vanilla extract

1–3 tablespoons ice water

Lightly grease a 9-inch pie pan, including rim. Dust with about 1 tablespoon unsweetened cocoa powder; set aside. In a food processor with a metal blade or in a medium bowl, combine 3 tablespoons of the cocoa powder, flour, sugar and salt. Add butter; process in food processor using quick ON/OFF pulses until mixture resembles coarse crumbs. *Or* use a pastry blender or 2 knives to cut butter into dry ingredients. Add vanilla and about 1½ tablespoons water; process with quick ON/OFF pulses (or stir) just until dough begins to hold together. Add additional water only if necessary. Form dough into a ½-inch-thick disk; let rest 5 minutes. If dough is very soft, chill 30 minutes.

Break dough into pieces and press over bottom and up sides of prepared pan. Form raised edge; crimp decoratively. Using a fork, prick shell at ½-inch intervals. Refrigerate for 30 minutes or freeze for 15 minutes.

Preheat oven to 425°F. Bake 10 to 12 minutes, or until crisp. Cool on a rack before filling.

Always serve too much hot fudge sauce on hot fudge sundaes.
It makes people overjoyed, and puts them in your debt.

—Judith Olney

Cookies 'n' Cream Crust

This super-easy crust contains less fat than most crumb-crust recipes and no added sugar because the cookies provide most of the sweetening.

Makes 1 (9-inch) piecrust

1¹/₂ cups Oreo or Hydrox cookie crumbs (about 22 cookies), including the filling (don't use cookies with double filling)
3 tablespoons butter, melted

Preheat oven to 350°F. Lightly grease a 9-inch pie pan. In a medium bowl, stir together cookie crumbs and butter. Turn mixture into prepared pan; with the back of a large spoon press firmly and evenly over bottom and up sides of pan. Bake 10 minutes; cool to room temperature.

Temperamental Temperatures

■ Oven temperatures can sometimes be off as much as 50° to 100°F, which can seriously affect baked goods. To check oven accuracy, place an oven thermometer on the center rack and preheat the oven for 15 minutes. If the thermometer reading doesn't agree with the oven setting (for example, if it reads 400°F when the oven is set at 350°F), you know that your oven runs 50°F hot. Therefore, when a recipe requires a 350°F temperature, set your oven to 300°F.

■ Most ovens have hot spots, which are easily detectable by how foods brown in them. To ensure even baking, rotate baking dishes and pans from top to bottom, and from front to back.

Chocolate Cups

These simple, edible chocolate containers can be filled with all manner of delectables including Marshmallow Whip (page 64), Black Magic Mousse (page 16), Almost-Instant Vanilla Silk (page 70) or a simple mélange of fresh berries topped by a puff of whipped cream.

Makes 8 to 12 cups

16–24 fluted foil or paper baking cups
8–10 ounces semisweet, sweet or white chocolate, melted and slightly cooled

Place 1 baking cup inside another, forming a double thickness. Using the back of a kitchen teaspoon, spread melted chocolate over bottom and up sides of paper cups. Push chocolate into ridges; smooth inside as evenly as possible. Chocolate should be about $1/8$ inch thick. As each baking cup is coated, place in muffin-pan cup to support sides. Refrigerate 15 minutes, or until chocolate is firmly set.

Check cups, repairing any thin spots with a dab of additional melted chocolate; chill to set. Carefully peel off paper or foil. Handle quickly and carefully—the heat of your hands can melt the chocolate. Cover and refrigerate chocolate cups for up to a month.

■ **Black and White Cups:** Use half white chocolate, half dark chocolate. Spread melted white chocolate over half of the bottom and sides of paper cups; refrigerate to set. Spread remaining half with melted dark chocolate; refrigerate until set.

■ **Miniature Chocolate Cups:** Use 60 ($1^1/2$-inch) miniature paper cups. Place 1 paper cup inside another, forming 30 cups with a double thickness. Proceed as for large cups. The tiny size of these cups makes them particularly vulnerable to the heat of your hands. Remove only 4 to 5 cups from the refrigerator at a time; carefully peel off paper. Return to refrigerator while working on remaining cups.

Chocolate Whipped Cream

Great on cheesecakes, pies, cakes and even warm fruit desserts like Chocolate-Cherry Clafouti (page 20).

Makes about 2 cups

2 tablespoons unsweetened cocoa powder

2–4 tablespoons confectioners' sugar

1 cup whipping cream

1 teaspoon pure vanilla extract

1–3 tablespoons Kahlúa, Grand Marnier
    or other liqueur (optional)

In a small mixing bowl, stir together cocoa powder and 2 tablespoons of the confectioners' sugar until thoroughly mixed. Slowly stir in whipping cream. Taste; add more sugar, if necessary (when using liqueur, allow for the sweetness it adds). Cover and refrigerate for 30 minutes.

Beat cream until it forms soft mounds. Beating constantly, add vanilla and, if desired, gradually drizzle in liqueur. Beat until liquid is incorporated and cream reaches desired consistency.

■ **Mocha Whipped Cream:** Add ½ tablespoon instant espresso (or 1 tablespoon instant coffee granules) to cocoa powder in first step. Increase sugar to 1 to 2 tablespoons.

Whipped Cream Options

■ *Lightened whipped cream:* Beat 1 or 2 room-temperature egg whites with $1/4$ teaspoon cream of tartar until stiff but not dry. Fold into 2 cups whipped cream (1 cup before beating) until thoroughly combined.

■ *Whipping cream ahead of time:* Beat cream until stiff, then spoon it into a sieve lined with a double layer of cheesecloth. Set over a bowl with the bottom of the sieve 2 inches above the bottom of the bowl. Cover tightly and refrigerate for up to 48 hours. If cream becomes too stiff, whisk in 1 to 2 tablespoons liquid cream.

■ *Stabilized whipped cream* (used for frosting cakes) won't soften and soak into cakes as readily as regular whipped cream: In a small bowl, stir 1 teaspoon unflavored gelatin into 3 tablespoons of water (or liqueur or fruit juice); set aside 5 minutes to soften gelatin. Place the small bowl in a pan of very hot water; stir mixture until gelatin is completely dissolved. Cool to room temperature. Beat 1 cup of whipping cream until soft peaks form. Beating constantly at medium-high speed, gradually drizzle cooled gelatin mixture into whipped cream. Use immediately to frost cakes; mixture sets quickly and becomes difficult to spread.

Whipped Cream Wisdom

■ Regular whipping cream contains 30 to 36 percent fat; heavy cream (also called heavy whipping cream) has a fat content between 36 and 40 percent.

■ Ultrapasteurized cream has been briefly heated at temperatures up to 300°F to kill the microorganisms that cause milk products to sour. It has a longer shelf life than regular cream but doesn't whip as well and has a slightly "cooked" flavor.

■ Refrigerate cream in the coldest part of the refrigerator. Most creams will keep at least a week past the date on the carton.

■ Freeze cream in its cardboard container (double wrapped in a freezerproof plastic bag) for up to 6 months. Defrost in the refrigerator overnight; shake well before using.

■ 1 cup whipping cream yields 2 cups whipped cream.

■ The bowl in which you whip cream should be deep enough so the cream can double in volume. Less than a cup of cream will whip faster in a deep, narrow bowl than one that's large and wide.

■ Cream will whip faster if it's very cold and if you put the beaters and bowl in the freezer for 15 minutes beforehand.

■ Get more volume by waiting until the cream forms soft peaks before adding sugar or flavoring such as vanilla or liqueurs.

■ Confectioners' sugar is generally used to sweeten whipped cream because it dissolves quickly and helps stabilize the whipped cream (it contains cornstarch).

■ Very sweet desserts are better served with unsweetened whipped cream, which has a natural sweetness of its own.

■ Overbeating cream can give it an undesirable buttery texture. To fix this, gently whisk in additional cream, 1 tablespoon at a time. Don't beat the cream again or you'll be right back where you started.

■ Try serving whipped cream at the soft-peak stage with some desserts. When slightly soft, the cream makes gentle folds over fruit, cobblers, etc. This texture is often much more inviting than firmly beaten cream standing stiffly at attention atop a dessert.

■ If you pour whipping cream over berries or other fruit a few minutes before serving, the natural acid in the fruit will slightly coagulate the cream, making it extra thick and luscious.

■ *Don't throw it out!* Cover and refrigerate leftover whipped cream for up to 3 days—use dollops of it atop coffee for a luxurious way to begin or end the day. Or freeze it by lining a baking sheet with plastic wrap, on which you spoon dollops of whipped cream at 1-inch intervals. Freeze, uncovered, until firm. Transfer the solid whipped-cream mounds to a plastic bag, seal airtight and return to the freezer for up to 2 weeks. Remove and use the dollops as you need them atop desserts or coffee. The cream will be soft in 5 to 10 minutes; less time on coffee and hot desserts. If the cream isn't sweetened, you can use it to enrich soups, sauces and other dishes.

Chocolate Leaves

Chocolate leaves are so dramatic and gorgeous, and so-o-o easy that I had to include them in this book. You can use any kind of chocolate, from dark to milk to white—the amount needed depends, of course, on the size of the leaves. I've used everything from huge 6-inch-wide hibiscus leaves to small lemon leaves. Look for those with well-defined veins and leave at least ¼ inch of the stem attached. One caveat: The leaves must be scrupulously dry—a speck of moisture will cause the chocolate to seize and harden.

Chocolate leaves can turn an ordinary-looking dessert into a showpiece, and can garnish everything from cakes and pies to custards and mousses. Arrange a garland of tiny chocolate leaves around the perimeter of a cake or cheesecake, fan 3 to 5 larger leaves of graduating sizes in the center of a pie or cake, or top a berry parfait or sundae with a single chocolate leaf to which a berry is attached. Go to it, have fun and impress the devil out of your friends!

Makes 6 to 8 chocolate leaves

2 ounces chocolate, melted and slightly cooled

6–8 nonpoisonous, firm leaves (camellia, rose, citrus or hibiscus), stems attached, washed and thoroughly dried

Line a large baking sheet with waxed paper. Using the back of a kitchen teaspoon, a dull knife or a small metal spatula, thickly spread melted chocolate over underside of each leaf to within about ¹⁄₁₆ inch of the edge (don't coat the stem). The chocolate must be thick enough for it not to crack when you peel off the leaf. If some chocolate runs over the leaf edges, use your fingertip to remove it. Place leaves, chocolate side up, on prepared baking sheet. If coated leaves are too flat, position a teaspoon, upside down, under one or two to add visual interest. Refrigerate leaves until chocolate hardens, 10 to 15 minutes (pop them in the freezer if you're in a hurry). Hold chocolate-covered leaves up to the light to check for thin spots; use additional melted chocolate to patch where necessary; chill to set.

To remove leaf, grasp stem and gently peel it away from the chocolate. Work quickly and carefully so that the heat of your hands doesn't melt the chocolate. Discard leaves. Refrigerate chocolate leaves in an airtight container until ready to use.

■ **Chocolate Leaves with Berries:** Attach a fresh raspberry, blueberry or small strawberry to a chocolate leaf using a tiny blob of melted chocolate as "glue." Refrigerate to set.

The sweets I remember best were white and tubular, much thinner than any cigarette, filled with a dark chocolate filling. If I found one now I am sure it would have the taste of hope.

—Graham Greene

Chocolate Butter

A decadent mélange to melt on everything from biscuits to pancakes. Or make cinnamon toast by spreading a thin layer of chocolate butter, then sprinkling cinnamon-sugar on top and broiling until bubbly. M-m-m-m—what a way to start the day!

Makes about ³/₄ cup

¹/₂ cup butter, softened

2 ounces semisweet chocolate, melted and cooled

2–4 tablespoons confectioners' sugar

1 teaspoon pure vanilla extract

In a medium bowl, beat together butter, chocolate and sugar to taste. Add vanilla, stirring to incorporate. Cover and refrigerate. Let stand at room temperature 20 to 30 minutes before serving.

Chocolate Decorations

■ *Chocolate curls:* To make curls, use a large, long bar of room-temperature chocolate; if chocolate is cold, shavings will be brittle and break. Hold wrapped chocolate firmly in your hand to warm slightly or place in a warm location (90°F) for about 15 minutes. Place a piece of waxed paper on work surface. Holding chocolate in one hand, and using a swivel-blade vegetable peeler in the other, firmly draw the blade toward you along the edge of the chocolate bar. The pressure you apply will determine the thickness of the curl. Let curls drop onto waxed paper. Refrigerate in an airtight container until ready to use. Use a spoon to gently transfer chocolate curls to desired dessert.

■ *Chocolate scrolls:* Line a large baking sheet with waxed paper. Melt 6 ounces of chocolate. Pour onto a smooth work surface, such as marble, Formica or the back of a baking sheet. Use a narrow metal spreading spatula to spread chocolate about $1/8$ inch thick over work surface. Let chocolate cool until firm but not hard. Starting at one end of chocolate and at side closest to you, use a flexible pastry scraper or wide metal spatula tilted at a 45-degree angle to slowly and firmly move spatula forward. The spatula edge will lift the chocolate and cause it to roll around itself. Use spatula to gently transfer chocolate scrolls to prepared baking sheet; refrigerate until firm, and store in an airtight container in refrigerator until ready to use.

■ *Chocolate triangles:* Line a large baking sheet with waxed paper. Draw an 8- or 9-inch circle on waxed paper. Spread 3 ounces of melted chocolate evenly within circle. Refrigerate until almost set. Using a large, sharp knife, cut chocolate circle into 10 to 12 pie-shaped pieces. Refrigerate until completely set. Gently break triangles apart; peel away waxed paper, handling chocolate as little as possible. Refrigerate in an airtight container until ready to use.

■ *Chocolate cutouts:* Line a large baking sheet with waxed paper. Spread 2 ounces of melted chocolate $1/16$ to $1/8$ inch thick on prepared baking sheet. Refrigerate until almost set. With canapé cutters, small cookie cutters or a pointed knife, cut out desired shapes in chocolate. Refrigerate until completely set. Gently break shapes apart; peel away waxed paper, handling chocolate as little as possible. Refrigerate in an airtight container until ready to use.

■ *Chocolate leaves:* See page 48.

Vanilla

Like a host at a good party, vanilla encourages all the elements present to rise to the occasion and make their own contributions to the whole, without calling undue attention to itself.

—Richard Sax

For decades, dictionaries have been defining the term "plain vanilla" as something "simple, plain or ordinary. . . a plain-vanilla car being the most basic model, without any extras." As a confirmed chocoholic, I admit being among those guilty of thinking that vanilla ranked a pale second to the dark, seductive allure of chocolate.

I vividly remember, however, the moment when that thought was forever banished from my psyche. It was a gloomy, rainy February day. I was in bed with a horrible flu and couldn't bear the thought of food. In walked my dear husband, Ron, with a mug of warm milk—not, by any means, my favorite beverage. But this steaming potion was heady with the haunting aroma of vanilla laced with cinnamon. The perfumed fragrance of the vanilla milk seemed to infuse my spirit and revive my body, affecting me in a mysterious and intrinsic way, each sip seeming to comfort and renew. I remember being surprised at never before realizing that vanilla is as much a smell as it is a taste, its fragrance beckoning and seducing with sweet promise. Since that day of culinary epiphany it's been clear to me that the term "plain vanilla" is an oxymoron in the truest sense, for there is definitely nothing ordinary about the quiet comfort and sensuality of vanilla.

And there's definitely nothing ordinary about the vanilla bean itself. The long, thin seedpod is actually born from a luminous celedon-colored orchid that, among more than twenty thousand varieties, is the only one that bears anything edible. This incredible orchid originated in Mexico, and history suggests that the vanilla bean may have been used as a flavoring for over a thousand years.

Vanilla was cultivated and processed by the Aztecs, who learned the techniques from members of the Indian tribes they conquered. In 1519, when Hernando Cortés and his conquistadores arrived in the Aztec capital of Tenochtitlán, they were greeted cordially by the emperor Montezuma, who made an enormous error in judgment by believing the Spaniards to be descendants of the god Quetzalcoatl. Montezuma honored these "gods" with glittering gifts and served them the "drink of the gods," a honey-sweetened, vanilla-laced chocolate bever-

age called *xocolatl*. Sadly, although the Aztecs were smart enough to build an amazing empire and to appreciate vanilla as a powerful flavoring, they made a *major* mistake in trusting Cortés, who proceeded to take their empire, their riches and their ruler's life.

Along with myriad other Aztec treasures, vanilla was brought back to Spain where the long, thin pod became known as *vainilla* ("little scabbard"). Vanilla accompanied travelers to other European cities, where at first it was used only in perfumery. It was also reputed to have wide-ranging powers, from medicinal to aphrodisiacal, which no doubt is why vanilla took Europe by storm. By the second half of the sixteenth century, Europeans were also using vanilla to flavor chocolate. Some wealthy citizens, however, were more than casual fans of the singular flavor of vanilla. I say *wealthy* because at the time vanilla was so rare and expensive that only royalty and the very prosperous could obtain it. Indeed, Queen Elizabeth I is said to have been so fond of vanilla that in her declining years she decreed all her food be flavored with it.

The United States was introduced to vanilla by esteemed statesman and connoisseur Thomas Jefferson, who became a fan of the aromatic pod on a trip to France. Still, vanilla wasn't widely available to

Americans until the mid-nineteenth century. Although nowadays vanilla can be found in supermarkets everywhere, it is still relatively expensive because of the incredibly labor-intensive, time-consuming process by which it is obtained. In fact, when you read "How Vanilla Is Made" (below) it will be perfectly clear that we are all very lucky indeed to be able to obtain this exotic flavoring.

Today, vanilla is used in an infinite number of ways besides cooking. Its fragrance graces perfumes, cosmetics, room deodorizing spray and envelope glue. It's even used for psychological purposes. According to a recent research study at Memorial Sloan-Kettering Hospital in New York, patients undergoing an MRI reported that the vanilla scent used during the procedure reduced their anxiety and stress.

Culinarily, vanilla adds its unique magic to a multitude of sweet and some savory dishes. It has an almost mysterious ability to mellow and enhance the flavor of many foods—chocolate, as the Aztecs demonstrated, being its first and most likely its soulmate partner. No doubt about it, vanilla's role in the world of food is definitely that of a leading lady. It highlights the richness of eggs and butter, softens the acidity of fruits like oranges and pineapples, enhances the natural sweetness of grains in baked goods and cereals, accentuates many spices such as cinnamon and allspice, and has become an increasingly popular flavoring for coffee.

So let's not hear any more about "plain vanilla," for nothing about this tropical orchid fruit is ordinary. In truth, vanilla is the hands-down winner as the most universally loved flavor. Why? Most likely because its seductive aroma and complex flavor can at once be comforting and familiar while invoking an intensely sensual response.

How Vanilla Is Made

The saga for each vanilla bean begins on the day its mother orchid (*Vanilla planifolia,* reclassified as *Vanilla fragrans*) blooms. This is a momentous event because the blossom opens only one day a year and then just for a few hours.

Fortunately, all the flowers don't open at once. During this extraordinarily tight time frame, the flower must be pollinated—and by hand because this particular orchid has only two known natural pollinators (the Melipone bee and the hummingbird), neither of which can possibly handle the task by itself. Each day, the vanilla vines are checked carefully for blooms, with only the best flowers chosen for pollination. The blooming/hand-pollination process can last for up to 2 months.

After pollination, the fragile flower dies and in its place begins to grow a bananalike cluster of long, green seedpods that resemble plump green beans. These pods (destined to be vanilla beans) can take 6 weeks to reach full size (6 to 10 inches long), and 8 to 9 months after that to mature. They're handpicked just as their green color begins to turn yellow at the tip.

At this point the mature pods have none of vanilla's seductive flavor or fragrance. For that they need a 3- to 6-month, labor-intensive curing process that begins with a 20-second bath in boiling water to stop their ripening. Then they're laid out in the sun, where they become extremely hot. Late each afternoon the hot pods are wrapped in blankets and allowed to sweat overnight. Over a period of months of drying in the sun by day and sweating in blankets at night, the beans ferment, a process that develops their perfumed flavor. It takes about 5 pounds of freshly picked vanilla beans to produce 1 pound of dried beans. The final step in curing is to spread the seedpods in a single layer either on racks or on grass mats where they dry in the sun for about 2 months. The beans are then sorted and graded for market. The better grades of beans sometimes have a thin white frosting of natural vanillin crystals.

In the United States, the vast majority of vanilla is sold as extract, which is made by macerating chopped beans in a water-alcohol mixture. The process is often compared to that of percolating coffee, with the liquid continually pumped over and through the flavoring components until the flavor is extracted. This extraction can be done with cool (around 60°F) or hot (130°F) liquid. Although the heat processing is faster, it decreases the flavor slightly. Five to 40 percent sugar may be added to an extract. The sugar both smooths the flavor and assists in aging, which can take several months. As with wine, aging allows the flavor of vanilla extract to expand and mellow.

Types of Vanilla

Vanilla Beans

Madagascar or Bourbon vanilla beans come from Madagascar (off the southeast coast of Africa), the Comoro Islands (an archipelago in the Indian Ocean) or the island of Réunion (formally called Isle de Bourbon) in the West Indian Ocean. These three areas produce about 80 percent of the world's vanilla-bean supply and most of the vanilla imported by the United States. Madagascar beans are the thinnest of the three types of vanilla bean and have a rich, sweet flavor.

Mexican vanilla beans, which are considered by many to be the best, come from environs surrounding Veracruz, Mexico. Thicker than Madagascar beans, they have a smooth, rich flavor. They are, however, relatively scarce because most areas where the orchid thrives are now dedicated to oil fields and orange groves. (*See* "A cautionary note" in the following section on Vanilla Extracts and Flavorings.)

Tahitian vanilla beans are plumper, shorter and darker in color than the other two types of bean. They have an intensely aromatic, flowery aroma, but are not considered to be quite as flavorful as Madagascar or Mexican vanilla beans.

Vanilla Extracts and Flavorings

Pure vanilla extract must, in order to meet FDA standards, contain 35 percent alcohol and 13.35 ounces of vanilla beans per gallon. This brown liquid is richly fragrant and has an intense flavor. There can be a marked difference between brands, so taste them and compare (*see* "Buying extracts," page 59). There are *double-* and *triple-strength pure vanilla extracts* available primarily through special mail-order suppliers as well as some gourmet shops. Pure vanilla extracts that contain additives like sugar or coloring must declare so on the label. Products labeled "natural vanilla flavor" contain only pure vanilla extract. Although some manufacturers make single-variety (Madagascan, Tahitian or Mexican) extracts, the majority on the market are a blend of beans from various locations.

A cautionary note: Some Mexican vanilla products contain a potentially toxic substance called coumarin, a derivative of the tonka bean, often used in Mexico to "extend" vanilla products. Coumarin, which can cause internal bleeding, liver and kidney damage and possibly cancer, has been banned by the FDA. Although Mexican vanilla products are considerably cheaper than their U.S. counterparts, there's no way to know if they contain coumarin. The best safeguard is to buy these products only from a reliable source.

Pure vanilla essence is a distilled product that's so concentrated only a few drops are generally necessary to flavor food. It's available through mail order.

Pure (or natural) vanilla flavoring is also derived from vanilla beans but contains less than 35 percent alcohol and has a less intense flavor than pure vanilla extract.

Vanilla flavoring is a blend of pure and imitation vanilla substances.

Vanilla powder is the whole, dried bean, ground until powdery. When heated (as in baked goods or custards), the flavor doesn't evaporate as readily as that of vanilla extract. Vanilla powder is available in cake-decorating supply shops, some gourmet markets and through mail order.

Artificial and imitation vanilla extracts and flavorings are composed primarily of artificial flavorings (chemically treated paper-industry by-products or coal-tar derivatives). Many have a harsh quality that can leave a bitter aftertaste. Pure vanilla extract is more expensive than its imitation counterpart, but can't be beat for purity and delicacy of flavor.

Note on labeling: Vanilla descriptions on labels can be confusing. *Natural vanillin* is a substance intrinsic to the vanilla bean, whereas *artificial vanillin* is made from wood pulp by-products. Foods like ice cream or pudding that carry the label "natural vanilla flavoring" contain only pure vanilla extract. The words "vanilla flavoring" on the package mean that a blend of pure and imitation vanilla was used, whereas "artificially flavored" tells you it's entirely imitation.

See also the section titled "How Vanilla Is Made," page 55.

Tips on Working with Vanilla

Buying Vanilla

• ***Buying beans:*** Look for vanilla beans that are dark and supple—you should be able to wrap the bean around your finger. The best beans are coated with a light frosting of natural vanillin crystals. Most readily available commercial vanilla beans are Madagascar (or Bourbon-Madagascar); Tahitian and Mexican beans (as well as better grades of Madagascar) are more readily available through mail order.

• ***Buying extracts:*** There can be marked differences in flavor from one brand of vanilla extract to another (see section on "Types of Vanilla," page 57). To determine what you like, sample several brands. Because of the high alcohol content in vanilla extract, it's difficult to evaluate the true flavor when tasting it alone. A better way to discern flavor characteristics is to combine ¼ teaspoon of extract with 2 teaspoons of milk.

Storing Vanilla

• Vanilla beans should be wrapped tightly in plastic wrap, placed in an airtight jar and refrigerated. Stored in this way, they'll keep for at least 6 months.

• Vanilla extract can be stored indefinitely if sealed airtight and kept in a cool, dark place.

Using Your Bean (Cooking with Vanilla)

• 1 whole bean = about 1 tablespoon (3 teaspoons) pure vanilla extract; 1 (2-inch) length of bean = about 1 teaspoon pure vanilla extract

• To use vanilla beans, slit them lengthwise down the center and scrape out the thousands of minuscule seeds. These seeds can be added directly to foods such as ice cream mixtures, the shortening used for pastry dough, cake batters, sauces, etc.

• It's easier to remove the seeds if the pods are soft. To soften stiff pods, steam them for a minute or two, either in a steamer basket or a sieve set over boiling water. Cool the pod slightly before slitting and removing the seeds.

• The vanilla bean may also be used whole to flavor a sauce or custard.

• Don't throw out a vanilla bean that you've used whole to flavor a dish like custard. Simply rinse and dry it thoroughly and store it for future use. Discard the bean when the fragrance fades.

• Or put a faded-flavor bean in a food processor with granulated sugar; process until finely ground and use in recipes or to sprinkle over cookies or other baked goods before baking.

• Because over a third of a pure vanilla extract is alcohol, much of the flavor evaporates when the vanilla is added to a very hot mixture. For maximum flavor, slightly cool mixtures like custards before stirring in the vanilla.

• Love the smell of vanilla? So will your refrigerator. Put a few drops on a cotton ball, set it in a custard cup and put it at the back of a shelf. The next morning, all will smell sweet.

Vanilla Lover's Pie

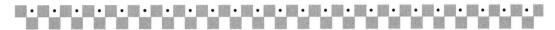

This caramel-cream dessert is ultra-rich and redolent with vanilla's heady perfume. Small portions are definitely in order. Here's a tip: The caramel will chill faster (which means the pie will be ready sooner) if you put the 2 cups of cream in the freezer about 30 minutes before stirring into the hot mixture.

Serves 10

¹/₂ cup light corn syrup

1 cup Vanilla Sugar (page 79) or plain granulated sugar

¹/₈ teaspoon salt

2¹/₂ cups whipping cream, divided

¹/₂ cup cold butter, cut into 8 pieces

1¹/₂ tablespoons pure vanilla extract

Vanilla-Nut Crust (page 62)

In a medium, heavy saucepan, combine corn syrup, sugar, salt and ¹/₂ cup of the cream. Cook over medium-high heat, stirring occasionally, until mixture reaches 230°F on a candy thermometer (a spoon coated with boiling syrup will form a 2-inch thread when immersed in a cup of cold water). Immediately turn caramel into a large mixing bowl. Add butter; beat until thoroughly combined. Stir in remaining 2 cups cream, then vanilla. Refrigerate until *very cold*—1 to 2 hours (length of chilling time depends on how cold the cream was to begin with). While filling is chilling, prepare and cool pie crust.

Whip chilled filling mixture until thick and fluffy. Turn into cooled crust, swirling top. Refrigerate until ready to serve.

The only way to get rid of a temptation is to yield to it.

—Oscar Wilde

Vanilla-Nut Crust

Although I created this crust for the Vanilla Lover's Pie (page 61), it's great for a myriad other concoctions, including Fudged Banana Cream Pie (page 82).

Makes 1 (9-inch) piecrust

*1¹/₂ cups fine vanilla wafer crumbs
    (about 36 cookies)*
¹/₂ cup minced walnuts or pecans
*¹/₄ cup Vanilla Sugar (page 79) or regular
    granulated sugar*
5 tablespoons butter, melted
1 teaspoon pure vanilla extract

Preheat oven to 350°F. Lightly grease a 9-inch pie pan. In a medium bowl, stir together all ingredients until well combined. Turn mixture into prepared pan; use the back of a large spoon to press firmly and evenly over bottom and up sides of pan. Bake 10 minutes; cool to room temperature.

■ **Chocolate-Nut Crust:** Substitute 1¹/₂ cups chocolate wafer crumbs for vanilla wafer crumbs; add 1 tablespoon unsweetened cocoa powder.

Greasing Pans the Right Way

■ Use vegetable shortening, unsalted butter or margarine, or nonstick vegetable spray to grease baking pans. Salted butter causes some baked goods to stick to pans.

■ Too much fat on a pan can cause overbrowning. So will salted butter at temperatures over 400°F.

■ The term "grease and flour" refers to sprinkling a greased pan with a small amount of flour, then tapping and rotating the pan or dish until the entire surface is coated with flour. Invert the container over the sink or wastebasket and shake it gently to remove excess flour.

■ Instead of "greasing and flouring" pans, use this homemade baker's magic: Beat until smooth $1/2$ cup each vegetable oil, room-temperature vegetable shortening and all-purpose flour. Refrigerate in an airtight container for up to 6 months and use as necessary to coat muffin tins, cake and bread pans, etc.

■ If you have trouble getting baked goods out of the pan, grease the pan, then line the bottom with waxed paper; then grease the waxed paper's surface. After the bread or cake is baked, and has been turned out of the pan, the waxed paper will peel right off.

Vanilla

Marshmallow Whip

Even though this dessert is almost fat-free, it gives the impression of being rich because of its intense sweetness, which means the servings can be small. Slightly tart fruit like raspberries or oranges make the best partners. A warning: If the marshmallow mixture sets during cooling, you'll have to remelt it—simply beating it won't bring back its original smoothness.

Serves 8

1 cup milk

1 (10 1/2-ounce) package miniature
    marshmallows

*5 egg whites, room temperature

1/2 teaspoon cream of tartar

1/4 teaspoon salt

1 tablespoon fresh lemon juice

1/4 cup sugar

1 tablespoon pure vanilla extract

About 2 cups raspberries or chopped fruit

*See "Do You Trust Your Eggs?," page 27

In a medium saucepan, combine milk and marshmallows. Cook over medium heat, stirring constantly, just until marshmallows are halfway melted. Remove from heat, stir until marshmallows are completely melted. Turn into a large bowl. Refrigerate, stirring often, just until mixture is barely cool (*don't let it set!*), 30 to 45 minutes.

In a large mixing bowl, beat egg whites until frothy. Add cream of tartar, salt and lemon juice; beat until soft peaks form. Beating continually, add sugar, 1 tablespoon at a time. Continue to beat until whites are glossy and firm; set aside.

Remove marshmallow mixture from refrigerator. Add vanilla, beating to incorporate. Stir in 1/3 of the meringue to loosen marshmallow mixture. Gently fold in remaining meringue, a third at a time.

Spoon into 8 small stemmed glasses. Cover and refrigerate for at least 1 hour before serving. May be made the night before. Just before serving, top with about 1/4 cup fruit.

Vanilla Bean Curd

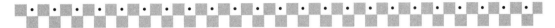

Inspired by the classic lemon curd, this recipe makes an enticing spread for hot biscuits, waffles and pancakes. Or you can double the recipe and use it as a filling for a fruit tart. Constant stirring is necessary during the last 5 minutes so the eggs don't become "scrambled." One tablespoon of pure vanilla extract can be substituted for the vanilla bean, if you prefer—add it just before you refrigerate the curd.

Makes about 1 cup

1 vanilla bean, split lengthwise in half

1/3 cup milk

1/4 cup sugar

1/4 teaspoon salt

3/4 cup unsalted butter, cut into 12 pieces

3 eggs, lightly beaten

Using a pointed spoon (a grapefruit spoon is perfect), scrape seeds out of vanilla bean pod.

Stovetop method: In the top of a double boiler, combine seeds and pod halves with milk. Over medium-low heat, bring milk just to the point where bubbles appear around the edge of the pan. Remove from heat; let stand 10 minutes. Use a slotted spoon to transfer pod halves to waxed paper; scrape a second time, returning seeds to milk. Discard pod. Stir in sugar, salt, butter and eggs. Set top of double boiler over bottom pan containing about 1/2 inch of simmering water (bottom of top pan should not touch water). Cook, stirring often during first 5 minutes. Then, stirring constantly, cook mixture until it is so thick that it almost mounds on itself.

Microwave oven method: Combine seeds and pod halves with milk in a 2-cup glass measure. Cook on high, uncovered, about 1 minute; let stand 10 minutes. Transfer pod halves to waxed paper; scrape a second time, returning seeds to milk. Discard pod. Add sugar, salt, butter and eggs. Cook on HIGH for 1 minute; stir. Cook on HIGH for 1 more minute; stir. Mixture will look clumpy.

continued

Turn hot mixture into a blender jar. With lid on, begin at low speed and gradually increase to high; process until mixture is creamy and smooth. Turn into a small bowl, stirring occasionally for about 5 minutes. Place a piece of waxed paper or plastic wrap directly on surface of curd, then cover container. Refrigerate overnight. Can be refrigerated for up to 5 days.

The Art of Beating Egg Whites

■ Eggs must be separated so that no yolk gets into the whites. Yolk contains fat, a single drop of which will prevent egg whites from reaching their full volume when beaten. Crack one egg at a time, placing each white in a custard cup before transferring it to the mixing bowl. This prevents any broken yolk from accidentally getting into the whites. If a speck or two of yolk does transfer, use a cotton-tipped swab or the corner tip of a paper towel to blot it up.

■ Eggs separate more easily when cold, but room temperature egg whites produce more volume when beaten. To quickly warm cold egg whites, set the bowl of whites in a larger bowl of warm water. Stir occasionally until whites have reached room temperature.

■ For beating whites until stiff, use a small, deep bowl with a rounded bottom for 4 to 5 egg whites; a large, deep bowl for more.

■ The composition of the bowl in which you beat egg whites can make a big difference. Copper bowls react chemically with egg whites to form fluffy, high-rise whites. The same result can be obtained using stainless steel or glass bowls with the addition of cream of tartar. The naturally slick surface of a glass bowl doesn't give as much traction for the egg whites to climb the sides. Never use aluminum (which can cause egg whites to turn slightly gray) or plastic or wooden bowls (which are hard to clean well enough so as to be free of fats or oils).

■ Adding a small amount of acid, such as cream of tartar, lemon juice or vinegar, stabilizes egg whites and allows them to reach their full volume and stiffness. The natural acid on the surface of a copper

I prefer vanilla in tradition-bound formulas
that maximize my sense of emotional comfort when I lick the spoon.

—Bert Greene

bowl achieves the same effect. Use $1/8$ teaspoon of the acid ingredient per egg white, except for meringues, where $1/8$ teaspoon is sufficient for 2 egg whites because of the added sugar. Add the acid to the whites just as they become frothy during beating.

■ Egg whites beaten without sugar will not peak as firmly as those beaten with sugar.

■ It's important to beat egg whites only until they're stiff but not dry—overbeaten whites will collapse and reliquefy.

■ If a recipe calls for the yolks and whites to be beaten separately, measure all the recipe ingredients out in advance, then beat the whites first and transfer them to a plate (properly beaten whites can afford to stand for a few minutes). The same bowl and beaters can then be used (without washing) to beat the yolks.

■ To fold stiffly beaten egg whites into another mixture, use a large rubber spatula to quickly, but gently, cut into the middle of the mixture, bringing the bottom of the batter up and over itself. Rotate the bowl a quarter turn with each folding motion. Fold gently to retain as much air as possible and stop folding as soon as the two mixtures are combined.

■ If folding stiffly beaten egg whites into a very thick or heavy mixture, first stir in about a quarter of the whites. This will loosen the mixture and enable the remainder of the whites to be folded in with ease.

Baked Vanilla Toast

The fragrance that fills the house when this dish is baking is like a giant, comforting hug. This recipe comes from my friend Olga Granovich, who learned it from her Armenian grandmother. Olga serves it for dessert, but it's equally wonderful for breakfast or brunch on a cold winter's day. I love this comfort food because it's extraordinarily simple and *totally* satisfying.

For this recipe, you'll need about a 10- to 12-ounce loaf of bread. Whether or not you remove the crust depends on how crisp it is and your personal preference. To make sure you have the right number of bread slices, fit them into the 9 × 13-inch pan before toasting them. Remember that bread shrinks slightly as it toasts. Although Olga makes her baked vanilla toast with French or Italian bread, when I make it for brunch, I often use a hearty wheat-nut bread.

Serves 6

12–14 (1-inch) slices French or Italian bread

1¹/₂ cups water

1¹/₂ cups whipping cream

1 cup plus 1 tablespoon sugar

¹/₂ teaspoon ground cinnamon

¹/₄ teaspoon salt

2 tablespoons pure vanilla extract

About 1 cup half-and-half or additional whipping cream (optional)

Preheat oven to 350°F. Arrange bread slices 1 inch apart on a large ungreased baking sheet. Bake until bread is crisp and golden, 15 to 20 minutes.

Meanwhile, combine water, 1½ cups cream, 1 cup sugar, cinnamon and salt in a medium saucepan. Cook, stirring occasionally, over medium-high heat until mixture comes to a boil. Remove from heat and let stand until toast is ready.

Lightly grease a 9 × 13-inch baking pan. Arrange toast slices over bottom of pan. Stir vanilla into cream mixture. Spoon 2 spoonfuls of hot mixture over each slice of toast; repeat process, then pour remaining mixture over all the toast. Bake 1¼ hours, or until all the liquid is absorbed.

Remove from oven and sprinkle tops of toasts with remaining 1 tablespoon sugar. Broil 5 inches from heat source until toast surfaces are browned and caramelized. Serve hot; pass a pitcher of cream as an accompaniment.

It is the simple things in life that are ofttimes the most cherished.

—Anonymous

Vanilla

Almost-Instant Vanilla Silk

Less than 5 minutes of effort produces a silky-smooth concoction with a flavor and texture that belies its simplicity. It's extremely rich, so the servings are intentionally small (1/3 to 1/2 cup). I use Guittard's Choc-au-Lait (also called "vanilla milk chips"), although there are other brands of vanilla chips available. During the summer, this dessert is particularly nice garnished with fresh blueberries or strawberries. At other times, use a single chocolate leaf or a drizzle of Black Satin Sauce (page 40), both of which can be made well in advance. To be really showy, serve vanilla silk in chocolate cups. Although this recipe doubles easily, it does have one idiosyncrasy—use anything lighter than whipping cream and it won't set properly.

Serves 4 to 6

1 cup whipping cream
12 ounces vanilla milk chips
3 tablespoons butter

1 tablespoon pure vanilla extract
Chocolate Cups (page 43), optional
Optional garnish: 1 cup fresh berries, or
    4 to 6 Chocolate Leaves (page 48),
    or Black Satin Sauce (page 40)

In a 2-cup glass measure, microwave cream on HIGH for 2 minutes, or just until mixture begins to boil. *Or* heat cream in a small saucepan over medium heat.

While cream is heating, combine chips and butter in a blender jar. Pour hot cream into blender jar all at once. Cover and process at low speed until chips melt and mixture is smooth, 30 to 45 seconds. Add vanilla; process 2 seconds to combine.

Pour mixture into 4 to 6 small (6-ounce) pot de crème cups, crème brûlée ramekins, custard cups or Chocolate Cups. Refrigerate, uncovered, for 2 hours. Cover with foil and continue to refrigerate until set, about 4 hours. Garnish as desired.

Vanilla Sugar Snaps

These super-thin, butter-crispy cookies are special enough for company. Plan at least a week ahead so you can prepare the fragrant Vanilla Sugar. If you don't have any vanilla sugar, use granulated sugar and increase the vanilla extract by 1/2 tablespoon.

Makes about 4 1/2 dozen cookies

1 cup butter, softened
2 cups granulated Vanilla Sugar
    (page 79)
1/2 teaspoon salt
1 tablespoon pure vanilla extract
1/2 cup sour cream
2 cups all-purpose flour

In a large mixing bowl, beat butter, 1 1/2 cups of the sugar, salt and vanilla together until light and fluffy. Add sour cream and flour alternately in 3 additions, blending well after each. Spoon dough onto the center of a 12-inch length of plastic wrap. Fold long sides of plastic wrap over dough. With palms, roll wrapped dough into a log 2 1/2 inches in diameter. Twist ends of plastic wrap to seal. Freeze or refrigerate until very firm, 1 to 4 hours.

Preheat oven to 350° F. Grease 4 large baking sheets; set aside. Fill a small bowl with cool water; set aside. Remove dough from refrigerator and unwrap. Cut chilled dough into 1/8-inch slices. Arrange 2 inches apart on prepared baking sheets. Lightly brush surface of cookies with cool water; sprinkle liberally with some of the remaining 1/2 cup Vanilla Sugar, being careful not to get any on baking sheet (it'll burn if you do).

Bake 11 to 15 minutes, or until edges are golden brown. Let stand on baking sheets 30 seconds before using a metal spatula to carefully transfer the fragile cookies to racks. Store in an airtight container at room temperature for up to 1 week.

continued

■ **Chocolate-Chip Sugar Snaps:** Add 1 cup miniature semisweet chocolate chips with flour. Cut refrigerated roll into ¼-inch slices (yield will be about 2 dozen cookies).

■ **Chocolate Sugar Snaps:** Increase sugar used in dough to 2 cups, add ½ cup cocoa powder, decrease flour to 1¾ cups. Sprinkle tops of cookies with coarse deco- rating or plain granulated sugar instead of Vanilla Sugar.

■ **Mocha Sugar Snaps:** Prepare as for Chocolate Sugar Snaps, adding 1 table-spoon instant espresso powder (or 1½ tablespoons instant coffee granules) to sour cream mixture about 5 minutes before combining it with the remaining ingredients.

Hot Tips on Baking Cookies

■ Always preheat the oven for 10 to 15 minutes before baking the cookies. When using glass baking pans (for bar cookies or brownies), reduce the oven temperature by 25°F.

■ Invest in a good oven thermometer for accurate temperature readings. The best type is a mercury oven thermometer, available in gourmet or kitchen-supply shops. The all-metal, spring-style thermometers found in supermarkets are unreliable if jolted or dropped.

■ All ovens have hot spots, so if you're baking more than one sheet of cookies at a time, ensure even browning by rotating the sheets from top to bottom and front to back halfway through the baking time.

■ Prevent overbaking by allowing for oven variances—check cookies a couple of minutes before the minimum baking time.

■ If you're baking successive batches of cookies and using the same baking sheet, let it cool to room temperature before reusing. Cookie dough that is placed on a hot baking sheet can begin to melt and spread, which will affect final shape and texture; the cookie bottoms can also overbrown. Lightly regrease the cooled baking sheet before reusing.

■ When baking several batches of cookies, speed the turnaround time by dropping dough (or placing cookie-dough cutouts) onto sheets of foil or parchment paper, which will be ready to slide right onto the cooled baking sheets.

■ Cool individual cookies on a rack. Cool and store bar cookies right in the baking pan. Crisp-style bars must be cut while warm—before they crisp—to keep them from crumbling, while soft bar cookies should be cooled completely before being cut.

■ All cookies should be completely cool before being stored or they'll "sweat" and become soggy.

Dream Cream

When I was a little girl, the highlight of my summertime afternoon was that magical hour when the "ice cream man" drove down the street where we lived, his music-box melodies tinkling a siren call that set my mouth watering. I would race up to his shiny white truck and breathlessly ask for a Dreamsicle, a heavenly fusion of vanilla and orange. I still love that flavor alliance and have re-created it here in this silky-smooth cream. Orange flower water, a fragrant distillation of bitter-orange blossoms, can be found in supermarkets in the spice section.

Serves 6

1 cup whipping cream
2 cups half-and-half
Finely grated zest of 1 large orange
1 teaspoon orange flower water
1 vanilla bean, split lengthwise in half
6 egg yolks
²⁄₃ cup sugar
¹⁄₄ teaspoon salt
¹⁄₂ cup flour
1 cup orange juice, room temperature
2 teaspoons pure vanilla extract
6 thin seedless orange slices
¹⁄₂ cup whipping cream, whipped and
    lightly sweetened

In the top of a double boiler, combine cream, half-and-half, orange zest and orange flower water. Scrape seeds out of vanilla bean; add seeds and pod halves to mixture in double boiler. Bring to a simmer over medium heat. Cover and simmer 30 minutes.

During last 5 minutes of cooking, combine egg yolks, sugar and salt in small mixing bowl; beat until thick and pale. Gradually beat in flour. Remove hot cream mixture from heat. Beating egg mixture constantly at low speed, slowly add 1 cup hot cream mixture. Place top of double boiler over simmering water. Slowly whisk remaining egg mixture back into hot cream mixture; add orange juice. Stirring constantly, cook until mixture thickly coats back of metal spoon. Strain through a fine sieve into a medium bowl. Refrigerate, stirring often the first hour to release steam and prevent skin from forming on surface. Stir in vanilla extract. Spoon into 6 stemmed glasses. Cover and refrigerate for at least 4 hours.

Up to 8 hours in advance, cut each orange slice halfway from outer edge to middle. Twist each side in opposite directions so it forms an S shape. Cover and refrigerate until ready to use. Top each serving with a dollop of whipped cream and a twisted orange slice.

She had a strong sweetish odor that all her rose water and soap could not subdue, an odor I loved because it made me think of warm custard.

—Isabel Allende, *Eva Luna*

Don't Throw Out Those Leftover Egg Whites!

■ Tightly cover and refrigerate leftover egg whites for up to 4 days.

■ Egg whites can be frozen for up to 6 months. The easiest way is to place 1 raw white in each section of an ice cube tray. Freeze, then pop the egg-white cubes out into a freezer-weight plastic bag. Thaw what you need overnight in the refrigerator. For those of you with automatic ice cube machines, inexpensive ice cube trays can be purchased at hardware or variety stores.

Frozen Champagne Chiffon

Simple but sophisticated, this make-ahead dessert combines vanilla and champagne in a soft-frozen gossamer cloud. Although true champagne comes only from the Champagne region in northeast France, there are a myriad other sparkling wines that will do this recipe justice. Just remember the age-old caveat: Never use a wine in cooking that you wouldn't drink by itself—if the flavor is bad, it will only get worse with cooking. When testing this recipe, I used everything from premium ice cream to 97 percent fat-free frozen yogurt, with equally delicious results, so let your waistline be your guide.

Serves 8 to 10

1 cup plus 2 tablespoons sugar
1 (750-ml) bottle dry champagne or other
   good-quality sparkling wine, divided
4 egg whites, room temperature
1/8 teaspoon salt
2 teaspoons pure vanilla extract

2 pints good-quality vanilla ice cream or
   frozen yogurt, slightly softened
1 pint fresh strawberries, hulled and
   coarsely chopped, or whole
   raspberries (optional)

Combine 1 cup sugar and 1 cup of the champagne in a medium saucepan. Cook over medium-high heat, without stirring, until mixture registers 240°F on a candy thermometer, or until a drop of syrup in a cup of cold water forms a soft ball that flattens of its own accord when removed.

While syrup is boiling, beat egg whites with salt until they form soft peaks. Beating continually, slowly drizzle hot syrup into egg whites. Beat about 2 minutes, or until meringue is no longer warm. Beat in vanilla.

In a large bowl, stir ice cream until it has the texture of softly whipped cream. Working quickly, stir in 1/3 of the meringue to loosen mixture. Gently fold in remaining meringue; it's okay if a few puffs of meringue remain. Spoon into stemmed glasses. Cover and freeze for 3 to 4 hours. If using strawberries or raspberries, combine fruit with 2 tablespoons sugar. Cover and refrigerate for up to 6 hours.

Before serving, let dessert stand at room temperature for 5 minutes. Top each portion with 2 tablespoons champagne and, if desired, fresh berries.

■ **Orange Champagne Spoom:** Sherbet converts this dessert to what the British call "spoom." Substitute 2 pints orange or lemon sherbet for the ice cream.

Champagne . . . takes its fitting rank and position [at a ball] amongst feathers, gauzes, lace, embroidery, ribbons, white satin shoes, and eau-de-Cologne, for champagne is simply one of the elegant extras of life.

—Charles Dickens

How Sweet It Is!

Make any fruit sweeter and juicier by sprinkling it with a tablespoon or two of granulated sugar. Toss fruit lightly, then let stand at room temperature 20 to 30 minutes, tossing once or twice during that time.

Vanilla Caramel Sauce

Rich and gooey, this easy sauce is wonderful drizzled over everything from ice cream to pound cake to pudding.

Makes about 2 cups

1¹/₃ cups packed light brown sugar

³/₄ cup whipping cream

³/₄ cup light corn syrup

¹/₃ cup butter

¹/₈ teaspoon salt

1¹/₂ tablespoons pure vanilla extract

In a medium, heavy saucepan, combine all ingredients except vanilla. Cook over medium-high heat, stirring occasionally, until mixture reaches 230°F on a candy thermometer (or until a spoon coated with boiling syrup forms a 2-inch thread when immersed in a cup of cold water). Remove from heat; cool 30 minutes before stirring in vanilla. Stir before serving warm or room temperature.

Cover and refrigerate leftover sauce for up to 2 weeks. To reheat: Stir over low heat until consistency desired. *Or* microwave on MEDIUM (*50 percent power*) for 1 to 2 minutes.

Vanilla Sugar

This delectably perfumed sugar can be used to garnish cookies, cakes and other baked goods, or in such preparations as whipped cream and Vanilla Sugar Snaps (page 71). I keep two batches of vanilla sugar on hand—one granulated and one confectioners'; the latter is a must for whipped cream and to sprinkle over French toast and waffles. And, listen, don't discard those beans after you've scraped out the seeds for a recipe—they'll flavor a jar of sugar just as well as whole beans.

Makes 1 pound

1 pound sugar (about 2¹/₄ cups
granulated, 3³/₄ cups confectioners')
2 vanilla beans

In an airtight container, combine sugar and vanilla beans, pushing the beans well down into the sugar. Seal tightly; let stand for 1 to 2 weeks, giving the container a shake 2 or 3 times during that period. The beans will flavor repeated batches of sugar; replenish the sugar as you use it. Replace the vanilla beans (or simply add new beans) every 4 to 6 months.

Did You Know

...that for centuries sugar, which came in large, solid loaves, was referred to as "white gold" because it was so scarce and expensive? Thankfully—particularly for those of us with a sweet tooth—sugar is no longer rare.

Homemade Vanilla Extract

Although many recipes suggest using vodka for homemade vanilla extract, I prefer the mellow sweetness of light rum; my second choice is brandy, though a good brand can be relatively expensive. Know that homemade vanilla extract rarely reaches the flavor potency of commercial brands. If you use it often, start a second batch when the first one's halfway finished.

Makes 1 cup

2 (6- to 8-inch-long) vanilla beans
1 cup light rum or brandy

Split vanilla beans lengthwise in half, then cut crosswise into thirds. Combine beans and rum in an airtight container. Let stand in a cool (room-temperature), dark place, shaking occasionally, for 3 to 4 weeks. Before using homemade extract in a light mixture, such as whipped cream, strain to remove seeds.

Chocolate
and Vanilla

Fudged Banana Cream Pie

This incredible pie delivers the double whammy of vanilla and a dark fudgy layer in the middle. It's also great without the crust. Simply spoon the pudding into stemmed glasses and drizzle with Black Satin Sauce (page 40).

Serves 8

1 recipe Chocolate Pastry Crust (page 41)
*   or Chocolate-Nut Crust (page 62)*
2 1/3 cups milk
1 envelope (1 scant tablespoon)
*   unflavored gelatin*
1 vanilla bean, split lengthwise in half
3/4 cup sugar
1/4 cup cornstarch
1/4 teaspoon salt
3 egg yolks
3 eggs
3 tablespoons cold butter, cut into 6 pieces
1 tablespoon plus 1 teaspoon pure
*   vanilla extract*

4 ounces semisweet chocolate, finely
*   chopped*
1 1/2 cups whipping cream, divided
2 medium ripe but firm bananas

Prepare and bake pie crust; set aside.

Pour 1/3 cup of the milk into a small bowl. Stir in gelatin; set aside 10 minutes to soften. Pour remaining 2 cups milk into a medium, heavy saucepan. Scrape seeds out of vanilla bean; add seeds and pod halves to milk. Bring to a simmer over medium heat, stirring occasionally.

In a medium bowl, mix sugar, cornstarch and salt. Lightly beat yolks and whole eggs together. Stir half of the eggs into the sugar mixture, whisking until thoroughly combined. Add remaining eggs, stirring to blend. Gradually whisk in 1 cup hot milk. Slowly whisk egg mixture back into remaining hot milk mixture. Cook over medium-low heat, whisking constantly, until custard is very thick, about 5 minutes. Remove from heat. Add softened gelatin; whisk 1 minute to dissolve.

Strain through a fine sieve into a medium bowl. Add butter, stirring until melted. Stir in 1 tablespoon of the vanilla extract.

Refrigerate, stirring often the first hour to release steam and prevent skin from forming on surface. Place a sheet of waxed paper directly on the surface of the pudding; continue to refrigerate until very cold and thick. Cooling time can take up to 3 hours. For faster chilling, place pudding in the freezer, but stir mixture often to make sure it doesn't freeze.

When filling is cold, combine chocolate and ½ cup of the cream in a 4-cup glass measure. Microwave on HIGH for 1 minute. Remove from oven and stir until mixture is smooth and creamy. *Or* combine chocolate and cream in a medium saucepan. Heat over medium-low heat, stirring often, until chocolate is *almost* melted. Remove from heat; stir until mixture is smooth. Stir remaining 1 teaspoon vanilla into chocolate mixture, blending well. Cool *just* until room temperature. The chocolate should be fairly free-flowing so it can be poured—overcooling will make it too thick. If that happens, reheat in the microwave oven for 5 to 10 seconds.

Whip remaining 1 cup cream until very stiff. Stir pudding to loosen; fold in whipped cream, a third at a time. Spoon half the filling into pie crust, smoothing surface. Pour all but about 2 tablespoons of the chocolate over filling, spreading it to the edges. Cut bananas lengthwise in quarters, then crosswise into ½-inch slices. Sprinkle banana chunks evenly over chocolate-topped filling. Spoon remaining filling over bananas, mounding in center and smoothing top. Drizzle remaining chocolate sauce in a decorative lacy design over top of pie. Refrigerate for at least 4 hours before serving.

Don't Ruin the Top!

Want to protect a pie or cake but lack a cake cover and don't want to ruin that beautifully decorated topping? Do this: Insert toothpicks at 4-inch intervals in the top (and sides, with a cake); lightly drape a sheet (or two if the dessert is large) of plastic wrap over the picks, tucking the wrap under the dish to seal as airtight as possible. You can also use foil, but it isn't as flexible as plastic wrap.

An egg is always an adventure; the next one may be different.

—Oscar Wilde

Savory Uses for Chocolate and Vanilla

Although both chocolate and vanilla are commonly used to flavor desserts and baked goods, they can also complement savory dishes. Following are just a few of the ways these classic flavors can add pizzazz to other dishes:

Unsweetened chocolate (solid baking squares or cocoa powder) contributes both color and a rich, husky flavor. Be judicious when adding chocolate to a dish; taste it after cooking for a few minutes. You can always add more but there's no way to remove it. The desired effect is one of mystery not a blatant smack in the mouth.

■   Mole sauce (a classic Mexican sauce)

■   Spicy or salty condiments from tapenade to eggplant caviar

■   Tomato sauce

■   Chilis, soups, stews and ragouts

■   Dark breads like rye and whole wheat

■   Coffee

Vanilla makes magic with all manner of foods. It can highlight and expand other flavors like chocolate, mellow acidic foods like citrus fruits and pineapple, accentuate the sweetness in grains and enhance everything from coffee to cinnamon. Try a soupçon of vanilla in some of the following dishes:

■   Creamed corn

■   Sauces for seafood, veal and poultry

■   Hot chocolate

■   Coffee

■   Hollandaise and béarnaise sauces

■   Salad dressings

■   Tomato sauces

■   Fruit compotes

■   Applesauce

Brownie Ice Cream Sandwiches

These thin, chewy brownies are great all by themselves, but make absolutely fabulous ice cream sandwiches. The secret is that the brownie stays chewy even when frozen. One caveat: Make sure that the pan you use isn't warped or so thin that it *will* warp with oven heat. If that happens, the batter will conform to the slope of the pan, becoming too thick at one end and too thin at the other, which means that the thin portion will be too crisp, the thick part too moist. Use the best-quality ice cream—inexpensive versions will be quick to melt and won't deliver the flavor the brownies deserve.

Makes 12 ice cream sandwiches

1¹⁄₄ *cups all-purpose flour*

¹⁄₂ *cup unsweetened cocoa powder*

1 cup packed light or dark brown sugar

¹⁄₂ *teaspoon salt*

1 teaspoon baking powder

¹⁄₂ *cup dark corn syrup*

¹⁄₄ *cup vegetable oil*

2 large eggs

1 tablespoon pure vanilla extract

²⁄₃ *cup finely chopped pecans, walnuts or almonds*

2 pints premium vanilla ice cream, slightly softened

Position rack in center of oven; pre-heat oven to 350°F. Generously grease a 15 × 10-inch jelly-roll pan; set aside. In a medium bowl, combine flour, cocoa powder, brown sugar, salt and baking powder. Mix well to break up any clumps in cocoa and brown sugar; set aside. In a 2-cup measure or small mixing bowl, combine corn syrup, oil, eggs and vanilla; lightly beat to combine. Stir into flour mixture, blending only until dry ingredients are moistened. Pour into prepared pan, spreading evenly; sprinkle surface with nuts. Bake 10 to 15 minutes, or until a toothpick inserted in the center comes out clean. Cool on a rack to room temperature.

Run a knife around edges of pan to loosen brownie; use a metal spatula to release bottom of brownie from pan. Invert uncut brownie sheet onto a cutting board. Cut in half crosswise. Place one half, nut side down, in the center of a piece of plastic wrap about 30 inches long. Spoon dollops of softened ice cream over surface of brownie; use a knife or a small metal spatula to spread ice cream evenly and all the way to the edges. Place second half of brownie, nut side up, on top of ice cream. Fold plastic wrap over large brownie sandwich, sealing securely. Freeze for 3 hours, or until very firm (timing will depend on freezer temperature).

Using a very sharp, thin-bladed knife, cut into 12 (about 2½-inch) squares, cutting 3 strips lengthwise and 4 strips crosswise. If using within 24 hours, place brownie ice cream sandwiches on a flat surface; seal airtight and freeze. *Or* wrap each ice cream sandwich individually with plastic wrap and return to freezer. Freeze for up to 2 weeks.

Fallen Angel Cake

Never fear—this cake was so named not because it literally "falls," but because upon tasting it my friend Vinnie Tonelli grinned and said: "Ohmigod, the chocolate in this cake could lead angels astray!" Besides the chocolate, this angel food cake is different in another major way: It contains baking powder, which helps boost the chocolate chips. Be sure to use miniature chocolate chips—regular-size chips are too heavy for the delicate batter. You can crown this tender, supermoist cake with a chocolate glaze, but it's perfectly wonderful served plain.

Serves 10 to 12

Cake

1 cup sifted cake flour

1 teaspoon baking powder

1½ cups superfine sugar, divided

10 egg whites (about 1½ cups), room temperature

½ teaspoon salt

1½ tablespoons pure vanilla extract

1½ teaspoons cream of tartar

⅔ cup miniature semisweet chocolate chips

Glaze

3 ounces bittersweet or semisweet chocolate, finely chopped

3 tablespoons whipping cream

1½ tablespoons butter

Position oven rack a third of the way up from bottom of oven. Preheat oven to 350°F. Set aside a 10-inch ungreased tube pan.

Cake

Sift flour, baking powder and 1/2 cup of the sugar together through a fine sieve 3 times. *Or* combine flour, baking powder and sugar in a food processor with the metal blade; process 30 seconds.

In a large mixing bowl, beat egg whites and salt at medium speed until frothy. Stop mixer; add vanilla and cream of tartar. Turn mixer speed to medium high; beat whites until they form soft peaks. Immediately begin adding remaining 1 cup sugar, 2 tablespoons at a time. Sprinkle sugar toward the bowl's side, scraping bowl as necessary. The whites should form medium-firm peaks that fold over softly; overbeating can cause the cake to fall slightly during baking.

Sift flour mixture over the meringue in 5 or 6 additions, and add about 2 tablespoons chocolate chips each time, gently folding after each addition. Using a large rubber spatula and a minimum of strokes helps retain body and diminishes deflation of the egg whites. Be careful not to overwork the mixture.

Gently spoon batter into prepared pan; smooth surface. Lightly cut through batter with a kitchen knife in a zigzag pattern to destroy any large air bubbles. Use the back of a spoon to gently smooth surface. Bake 35 to 40 minutes, or until surface just springs back when lightly pressed with your fingertip. Overbaking will cause the cake to fall. Immediately invert cake in pan onto a cake rack or over a narrow-necked bottle. Cool completely in pan.

Run a thin knife around pan between cake and side of pan; repeat with center tube. Turn cake out onto cake plate, rapping the pan bottom, if necessary, to release cake.

Glaze

Combine all ingredients in a 2-cup glass measure. Microwave on HIGH for 1 minute. Stir well. Microwave 30 seconds; stir until mixture is smooth and creamy. *Or* combine ingredients in a small saucepan. Heat over medium-low heat, stirring often, until chocolate is melted and mixture is smooth. Cool to room temperature. Spoon glaze over top of cake, allowing it to drizzle down sides. Let glaze set at least 20 minutes before serving.

Chocolate
and
Vanilla

Lofty Logic for High-Rising Angel Food, Chiffon and Sponge Cakes

■ Tube pans used for foam-type cakes like chiffon, sponge or angel food are never greased. The ungreased sides of the pan allow enough traction for the delicate batter to cling to as it bakes and then again as it cools.

■ Cake flour produces lighter cakes because it contains less gluten. If you don't have cake flour, substitute 1 cup stirred all-purpose flour, minus 2 tablespoons, for each cup of cake flour.

■ Although superfine sugar is preferred for sponge-type cakes, it isn't absolutely necessary. Create your own superfine sugar by processing an equal amount of granulated sugar in a food processor with a metal blade for 1 minute. In a pinch, simply use granulated sugar.

■ Eggs for cakes should be at room temperature. To quickly warm refrigerated eggs, place them in a bowl of very warm (but not hot!) water for 5 to 10 minutes. If separating the eggs, place the yolks in one bowl, the whites in another, and then set the separate bowls in a pan of warm water. Don't fill the pan so full that the water gets into the eggs.

■ Many foam-type cake recipes call for sifting flour and sugar together several times. If you don't have a sifter or fine sieve (or the patience), simply process flour and sugar together for 1 minute in a food processor with a metal blade.

■ Once the batter's in the pan, eliminate air bubbles, which would create holes in the cake, by running a knife in a zigzag pattern through the batter.

■ A chiffon, sponge or angel food cake is done when it springs back when lightly touched in the center with your finger.

■ Cool these cakes by inverting the pan; this keeps them from falling. Many tube pans have legs on which the pan can stand so air can circulate underneath. If yours doesn't have built-in legs, invert the pan and position the tube over a narrow-necked bottle.

■ Cooled angel food cake can be left in the pan, covered tightly with foil, for up to a day until you're ready to frost it.

■ To loosen a cake from a pan, use a long knife with a thin blade or a metal spatula (not a pancake turner). Press the knife or spatula firmly against the side of the pan and slowly rotate the pan until back to the starting point. It's important to keep the knife or spatula pressed against the pan so the cake doesn't tear. Foam-type cakes must be *thoroughly* cool before being removed from the pan or they will fall.

■ Angel food cakes "set" and are easier to slice if you freeze them, wrapped airtight, for 24 hours. Bring to room temperature before frosting.

■ Use a serrated knife for cutting delicate cakes. Soaking the blade in very hot water for a couple of minutes will facilitate cutting even more (be sure to dry off the knife).

■ *Troubleshooting:* If a chiffon, sponge or angel food cake hasn't risen sufficiently, it's probably due to one of three things: Either the egg whites were overbeaten—stiff but dry, rather than moist and glossy; or underbeaten and not stiff enough; or the batter was overmixed, rather than gently folded, as the flour was added. If the cake falls *after* it's baked, it could also be because the whites were overbeaten, or that the cake was cooled right side up, or that the cake was baked too long. Overmixing can also cause such cakes to be tough.

What to Do with All Those Leftover Egg Yolks

■ Save yolks that will be used within a day or two by sliding them into a small container of cold water; water should cover yolks. Seal airtight and refrigerate for up to 2 days.

■ If several broken yolks have run together, figure on 1 tablespoon plus 1 teaspoon yolk equaling 1 whole yolk.

■ Yolks that won't be used within 2 days can either be cooked or frozen. To cook, carefully place them into a small saucepan containing at least 1 inch of cold water. Bring to a boil; immediately remove pan from heat, cover and let stand for 15 minutes. Use a slotted spoon to remove cooked yolks from water. Cover and refrigerate for up to 5 days; or wrap airtight and freeze for up to 4 months.

■ Freezing uncooked yolks requires special attention because yolks become so gelatinous when frozen they're almost impossible to use. To inhibit gelatinization, add $1/8$ teaspoon salt or $1\frac{1}{2}$ teaspoons sugar or corn syrup to every 4 yolks; beat to combine. Whether you add salt or sugar depends on how you plan to use the yolks later on. Label the container as to what you used, and freeze for up to 3 months.

Chocolate and Vanilla

To-Die-For Caramel Brownies

What a way to go! Rich, fudgy, moist brownies topped with a shiny, chewy vanilla caramel loaded with toasted pecans. One of the best things about this recipe is that the brownies stand alone beautifully without the caramel topping—and I've created eight decadent variations on the theme.

Makes 2 dozen brownies

³/₄ cup butter, softened

2 cups packed brown sugar

1 cup granulated sugar

1 tablespoon pure vanilla extract

1 teaspoon instant espresso powder

¹/₂ teaspoon salt

6 ounces unsweetened chocolate, melted and cooled to room temperature

4 ounces semisweet chocolate, melted and cooled to room temperature

5 eggs

1¹/₂ cups all-purpose flour

Vanilla Caramel Sauce (page 78), with changes (see directions)

2 cups coarsely chopped toasted pecans

Preheat oven to 350°F. Grease a 9 × 13-inch baking pan; set aside. In a large mixing bowl, beat butter, sugars, vanilla, coffee powder and salt until well combined. With mixer running at medium-low speed, gradually add both melted chocolates, then eggs, one at a time, beating well after each addition. Stir in flour, ¹/₂ cup at a time. Spoon into prepared pan, smoothing top. Bake about 35 minutes, or until a toothpick inserted in the center comes out *almost* clean. Do not overbake. Cool in pan on a rack for 1 hour.

When brownies are almost cool, begin preparing Vanilla Caramel Sauce, cooking the mixture until it reaches *240°F* on a candy thermometer. Remove from heat; immediately stir in nuts, then the 1¹/₂ tablespoons vanilla called for in the caramel recipe. Immediately pour caramel over brownie base. Working quickly, use the back of a kitchen tablespoon to spread caramel in an even layer to edges of brownies. Cool completely in pan on a rack. Cut into 24 (about 2-inch) squares, cutting 6 strips crosswise and 4 strips lengthwise.

■ **Fudge-Nut Brownies:** Stir 1½ cups nuts into brownie batter; sprinkle remaining ½ cups nuts over surface of batter before baking. Omit caramel topping.

■ **Chocolate-Chunk Brownies:** Stir 1 cup chopped nuts and 8 ounces dark or white chocolate (chopped into ³⁄₈-inch chunks) into the brownie batter; omit caramel topping.

■ **German Chocolate Brownies:** Reduce brown sugar to 1 cup; substitute 6 ounces German's sweet chocolate for unsweetened chocolate. Add 1 cup flaked or shredded coconut and 1 cup pecans to batter; sprinkle top of batter with ⅓ cup coconut before baking. Omit caramel topping.

■ **Cookies and Cream Brownies:** Coarsely chop 30 Oreo or Hydrox cookies.

Fold all but 1 cup cookies into brownie batter; sprinkle reserved chopped cookies over surface before baking. Omit caramel topping.

■ **Fudge-Mint Brownies:** Omit coffee powder; add ½ to ¾ teaspoon peppermint extract with vanilla. Omit caramel topping.

■ **Mexican Chocolate Brownies:** Add 2 teaspoons ground cinnamon and ½ teaspoon each ground cloves, ground nutmeg and ground allspice to butter mixture before beating.

■ **Espresso-Fudge Brownies:** Increase instant espresso powder to 2 tablespoons. If omitting caramel topping, stir 1 to 2 cups nuts into batter.

■ **Cherry Brownies:** Omit coffee powder and caramel topping. Soak 1 cup dried cherries (sour or sweet) in very hot water to cover for 15 minutes to rehydrate. Drain and thoroughly blot dry. Stir cherries into batter; if desired, add 1 cup chopped nuts.

Give me the luxuries of life and I will willingly do without the necessities.

—Frank Lloyd Wright

S'more Pie

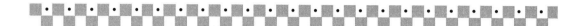

I created this pie at the request of my twelve-year-old nephew, Andrew Leslie. I've since discovered, however, that kids of all ages love it—no doubt because it brings back fond memories of sitting around the campfire after a day of outdoor fun. You can shortcut this super-easy, 4-ingredient recipe by using a storebought crust. If you use the crust recipe here, note that it contains (purposefully) no sugar; the filling is plenty sweet on its own. Baking the crust first delivers a much crisper end product than just pressing the mixture into the pan and refrigerating it. To replicate that campfire feeling, broil the marshmallow topping just before serving the pie. It'll be runny but it'll be *good*. Even after the pie's been refrigerated several hours the topping will still be deliciously soft.

Serves 8 to 10

Crust
1¹/₂ cups graham cracker crumbs
6 tablespoons butter, melted

Filling
1¹/₂ cups whipping cream
12 ounces semisweet or milk chocolate,
 finely chopped
2 teaspoons pure vanilla extract
2 (7-ounce) jars marshmallow creme

Crust
Preheat oven to 350°F. Butter a 9-inch pie pan. In a medium bowl, combine crust ingredients; turn into pie pan. Use the back of a large spoon to press the mixture firmly and evenly over bottom and up sides of pan. Bake 10 minutes. Cool completely before filling.

Chocolate
and
Vanilla

Filling

In a 4-cup glass measure, combine cream and chocolate. Microwave on HIGH for 1½ minutes; stir well. Microwave 1 more minute; stir until mixture is smooth and creamy. (Mixture may require an additional 30 seconds of heating, depending on the microwave wattage.) *Or* combine cream and chocolate in a medium saucepan. Heat over medium-low heat, stirring often, until chocolate is melted and mixture is smooth. For either method, stir vanilla into melted chocolate mixture, blending well. Pour into cooled crust; refrigerate for at least 4 hours.

Position rack 4 inches from broiling unit; preheat broiler. Spoon dollops of marshmallow creme over surface of pie. Gently spread over surface to within 1 inch of edge of crust (marshmallow will spread when heated). If you're using a glass pie plate, place pie in the middle of a 10 × 15-inch jelly-roll pan; surround plate with ice cubes. This will prevent the broiler heat from cracking the cold pie plate; it's not necessary to do this with a metal pan. Broil pie until marshmallow surface is browned to your liking, turning the pan as necessary for even heat. Serve immediately or refrigerate until ready to serve. Use a serrated blade (a tomato knife is perfect) to decrease cracking when you cut through the thin layer of crispy toasted marshmallow.

Once in a young lifetime one should be allowed to have as much sweetness as one can possibly want and hold.

—Judith Olney

Black Bottom Crème Brûlée

The hidden attraction in this delectable dessert is a rich, dark fudgy sauce that appears as your spoon reaches the bottom of the creamy vanilla-bean custard. Because the fudgy black bottom adds richness, I've lightened the classic custard by replacing whole eggs for some of the egg yolks and substituting half-and-half for some of the whipping cream. If you don't have a vanilla bean on hand, stir in 1 tablespoon pure vanilla extract after the custard cools.

Serves 6

Black Bottom

1/4 cup unsweetened cocoa powder

1/2 cup sugar

Pinch of salt

1/3 cup plus 1 tablespoon whipping cream

1 tablespoon butter

1/2 teaspoon pure vanilla extract

Custard

1 vanilla bean, split lengthwise in half

2 cups whipping cream

1 cup half-and-half

2 large eggs

2 large egg yolks

1/3 cup sugar

1/8 teaspoon salt

1 teaspoon pure vanilla extract (optional)

About 3/4 cup packed light brown sugar

Black Bottom

In a small, heavy saucepan, combine cocoa powder, sugar and salt; stir until cocoa is no longer lumpy. Gradually stir in cream. Bring mixture to a boil over medium-low heat, stirring constantly. Reduce heat to low; cook 2 minutes, stirring constantly. Remove from heat. Add butter, stirring until melted. Stir in vanilla. Divide evenly between 6 (6-ounce) custard cups, soufflé dishes or crème brûlée ramekins (about 1½ tablespoons per dish). Place dishes in freezer until custard is ready.

Custard

Using a pointed spoon (like a grapefruit spoon), scrape seeds out of vanilla bean pod. Add seeds and pod halves to cream and half-and-half in the top of a double boiler. Over medium-low heat, stirring occasionally, bring cream just to a simmer. Remove from heat; let stand 10 min-utes. Use a slotted spoon to transfer pod halves to a flat work surface; scrape a second time, returning seeds to cream. Discard pod.

While cream is standing, place eggs, egg yolks, sugar and salt in a small mixing bowl. Beat until thick and pale. Gradually whisk 1 cup hot cream into egg mixture. Stir mixture back into remaining hot cream in pan. Place top of double boiler over simmering water. Stirring constantly, cook 10 to 15 minutes, or until mixture *thickly* coats back of metal spoon. Remove from heat; strain through a fine sieve into a medium bowl. Place bowl in a larger bowl of ice water. Stir occasionally until custard is room temperature. Taste; add vanilla, if desired. Gently spoon cooled custard over chocolate sauce, dividing evenly among dishes. Cover and refrigerate for 8 hours or overnight.

Two to three hours before serving, preheat oven broiler, positioning rack so that top of custards will be 6 inches from heat source. Using the back of a spoon, rub brown sugar through a sieve with a medium mesh over surface of custards, topping each serving with an even layer no thicker than $1/8$ inch. Set custard dishes in a 9 × 13-inch baking pan; surround dishes completely with ice (to keep the glass dishes from cracking from the broiler heat). Place under heat source; broil until sugar begins to melt, caramelize and form a hard crust, 3 to 5 minutes. Watch very carefully, turning dishes if necessary to prevent sugar from burning. Cool 15 minutes, then refrigerate for up to 5 hours before serving.

Getting Stirred Up About Custards

■ Don't try to hurry stirred custards by raising the heat—you'll only succeed in curdling the mixture.

■ If your custard begins to curdle, pour it into a blender jar, cover and process until smooth (start the blender at low speed and gradually increase to high). Clean the pan of any residue, then return the custard to the pan and begin cooking again.

■ A stirred custard is done when it leaves a velvety-thick coating on the back of a metal spoon. Run your finger across the spoon; if it leaves a definitive track, with a thick coating of custard clearly defined on either side, the mixture's ready.

■ Another way to test a custard is to insert a candy thermometer in it. If the temperature registers 165°–170°F, the custard's ready.

■ Remove the custard from the heat as soon as it's done. Overcooking causes egg-based mixtures to curdle and separate.

■ To make sure the finished custard is silky smooth, pour it through a fine sieve into a bowl.

■ You can quickly cool a stirred custard by placing the pan in a large bowl of ice water. Stir the custard constantly until it reaches the desired temperature.

■ Once the custard has cooled to room temperature, immediately cover the surface with waxed paper or plastic wrap (put it right on the surface) and refrigerate. The custard will become slightly thicker when cold.

■ All egg custards should be refrigerated, covered and consumed within 3 days.

Seriously Sinful Shortbread

Half chocolate, half vanilla, these delicate, buttery cookies make a perfect ending to any meal and a great teatime accompaniment.

Makes about 2¹/₂ dozen cookies

1 cup butter, softened

1 cup confectioners' sugar

1 tablespoon pure vanilla extract

¹/₄ teaspoon salt

1³/₄ cups all-purpose flour

¹/₄ cup unsweetened cocoa powder

¹/₄ cup grated semisweet chocolate

In a large mixing bowl, beat butter, sugar, vanilla and salt at medium-high speed until light and fluffy. In a medium bowl, add 1 cup of the flour; stir in half the butter mixture (1 slightly rounded cup), blending until combined. In another medium bowl, combine remaining ³/₄ cup flour, cocoa powder and grated chocolate. Stir in remaining butter mixture, blending until well combined. Both doughs will be extremely soft.

Spoon the chocolate dough in a 12-inch log lengthwise down the center of a 18-inch length of plastic wrap. Spoon vanilla dough right next to and touching the chocolate dough. Fold long sides of plastic wrap over doughs, pressing the two together. Twist ends of plastic wrap to seal. Use your fingers to gently compress the log so the doughs are well attached. The finished dough log should still be 12 inches long. Refrigerate until firm, 1 to 2 hours.

Preheat oven to 300°F. Place dough log on a cutting board, *chocolate side down.* Use a sharp, thin-bladed knife to cut log into ³/₈-inch slices. Place slices 1 inch apart on ungreased baking sheets. Bake 15 to 20 minutes, or until shortbread is set (cookies won't brown). Let stand on baking sheet for 3 minutes. Use a metal spatula to carefully transfer cookies to racks; cool completely. Gentle handling is necessary as shortbread is very delicate.

Shortbread has beneficial effects on the soul. The warm glow it gives is better than alcohol, and more readily available than sex.

—Lucy Ellman, *Sweet Desserts*

The Bottom Line on Baking Sheets and Pans

■ Shiny heavy-gauge aluminum baking sheets are good heat conductors and produce the most evenly baked and browned cookies.

■ Dark sheets absorb more oven heat and can cause cookies to overbrown or burn. Lining dark sheets with heavy-duty aluminum foil alleviates the overbrowning problem.

■ Insulated baking sheets—two sheets of aluminum with an air pocket sealed between them—are fine for soft cookies, but cookies won't get as crisp when baked on them. Cookies may also take 1 to 2 minutes longer to bake.

■ Thin, lightweight baking sheets often cause cookies to burn. Stack two together to create more insulation.

■ Always use the pan size called for in a bar-cookie or cake recipe. A smaller pan, and the finished product will be too thick and gummy in the middle; a larger one, and the results will be thin and dry.

■ When using glass baking pans, reduce oven temperature by 25°F.

■ Save on cleanup by lining the baking sheets or pans with foil, leaving some overhang on each end. Grease the foil if called for. Once the cookies are baked and cooled, use the overhang to lift the cookie slab out of the pan, then cut into bars or squares. Transfer sheet-baked cookies from foil to a cooling rack.

■ Use vegetable shortening, nonstick vegetable spray, or unsalted butter or margarine to grease baking sheets and pans. Salted butter or margarine may cause cookies to stick and overbrown on the bottom.

■ Overgreasing baking sheets can cause cookies to spread and overbrown on the bottom.

■ Unless the cookie dough requires refrigeration, grease baking sheets before you begin mixing the dough.

■ Greasing baking sheets is usually unnecessary with high-fat cookies like shortbread.

■ To flour greased baking sheets, sprinkle the surface with about $1/2$ tablespoon flour; tap and rotate the sheet until the entire surface is coated with flour. Invert sheet over the sink and shake to remove excess flour.

Cookies 'n' Cream Cheese Torte

This easy and delicious torte goes together in minutes, and there's absolutely no baking, except for the crust, which you don't have to bake if you don't mind a soft crust. Use a sharp knife rather than a food processor to chop the cookies that will be folded into the filling—the chunks, though irregular, should be about 1/2 inch in diameter. A food processor will, unfortunately, produce more crumbs than chunks.

Serves 10

1 (1-pound) package Oreo or Hydrox
    cookies (not with double filling)
3 tablespoons butter, melted
2 (8-ounce) packages cream cheese,
    softened
1/2 cup sugar
1 tablespoon pure vanilla extract
1 cup whipping cream, whipped until stiff

Preheat oven to 350°F. Lightly oil a 9-inch springform pan; set aside. In a food processor with a metal blade, process 20 cookies until finely crushed. Add melted butter; process to combine. Turn into prepared pan. Use the back of a large spoon to press crumb mixture firmly and evenly over bottom of pan. Bake 10 minutes; cool to room temperature. For unbaked crust, simply refrigerate until ready to fill.

Reserve 10 cookies for garnish. Coarsely chop remaining cookies; set aside. In a large mixing bowl, beat cream cheese, sugar and vanilla, scraping bowl as necessary, until perfectly smooth and very fluffy. Fold in whipped cream, then chopped cookies. Turn into prepared crust; smooth top. Cover and refrigerate for least 3 hours.

About an hour before serving, remove side and bottom of pan; transfer torte to a serving dish. Position the 10 reserved whole cookies, evenly spaced and at a 45-degree angle, on top of cheesecake, pressing down slightly to anchor. Refrigerate until serving time.

*Chocolate
and
Vanilla*

Tunnel of Fudge Cheesecake

This rich vanilla cheesecake with a decadently dark tunnel of chocolate running through the center is a real show-stopper. My inspiration was a regular cake (made with a packaged frosting mix) that was a 1966 Pillsbury BAKE–OFF® Contest winner. I created this cheesecake for a dessert cooking class I gave 10 years ago and have been baking it ever since.

Serves 10 to 12

Cookies 'n' Cream Crust (page 42)
5 (8-ounce) packages cream
cheese, softened
1¹/₂ cups sugar
5 eggs
¹/₄ cup all-purpose flour
¹/₂ teaspoon salt
¹/₄ cup whipping cream
3 ounces semisweet chocolate, melted
and cooled
¹/₂ cup semisweet chocolate chips
1 tablespoon pure vanilla extract

Chocolate Whipped Cream (page 44) or
regular whipped cream, sweetened
to taste
5–7 Chocolate Leaves (page 48), optional

Prepare and cool crust. Preheat oven to 400°F. In a large mixing bowl, beat cream cheese and sugar together until smooth and fluffy. Add eggs, one at a time, beating well after each addition. Beat in flour, salt and cream. Place 2 cups of the cheese mixture in a medium bowl. Stirring constantly, gradually add melted chocolate, blending until well combined. Stir in chocolate chips; set aside. Stir vanilla into remaining cheese mixture.

Pour all but 1¹/₂ cups light cheese mixture into prepared crust. Spoon chocolate-cheese filling in a 2-inch-wide ring onto light cheese mixture, about 1¹/₂ inches from edge of pan. Be careful not to get any in center of light mixture. Using the back of a spoon, carefully press chocolate mixture down into light mixture until top is level. Spoon reserved light cheese mixture evenly over all; smooth top.

Place cheesecake in center of middle oven rack. Position a 13 × 9-inch baking pan filled halfway with hot water on lower shelf. Bake 15 minutes. Reduce heat to 300°F; bake additional 50 minutes. Turn oven off. Let cheesecake cool in oven 1 hour with oven door propped open 1 to 3 inches. Remove cheesecake from oven to a rack; cool completely. Cover and refrigerate overnight.

To complete cheesecake: Run a thin knife around inside edge of pan; remove side of pan. Use a thin knife to loosen crust from bottom of pan. With two large metal spatulas, carefully slide cheesecake off pan bottom onto a serving plate. Spread Chocolate Whipped Cream or regular whipped cream over top of cheesecake. Fan Chocolate Leaves in center of cheesecake. Chill for at least 1 hour before serving.

Too much of a good thing can be wonderful.

—Mae West

Cheesecake Know-how

- Cheesecakes require a delicate balance of ingredients, particularly eggs, cheese and liquid. Making major substitutions can drastically alter the final product.

- It's essential to use the size pan specified in a cheesecake recipe.

- Add and blend cheesecake ingredients in the precise order given in a recipe.

- Before beginning to mix the cheesecake, position the oven rack in the middle of the oven; preheat oven 15 minutes. Use an oven thermometer for accurate oven temperature.

- Cracks are a common problem for which there are several reasons. One is that as a cheesecake bakes, its moisture evaporates. If too much moisture is lost or if it evaporates too quickly, cracking will occur on the cheesecake surface. To alleviate this problem, increase the oven humidity by placing a shallow pan of hot water on the bottom shelf before preheating.

- Prebaking a crumb crust helps keep it crisp. Completely cool before filling.

- For a moisture-proof seal on a prebaked crumb or pastry crust, spread 2 to 3 ounces of melted semisweet chocolate over the crust's surface to within ¼ inch of the outside edge. Refrigerate the crust for about 10 minutes to set the chocolate before filling with the cheesecake mixture.

- The cheese should be at room temperature so it's easier to blend with other ingredients.

- Always beat cream cheese until light and fluffy before blending in other ingredients such as eggs.

- Ricotta and cottage cheese–style cheeses should be beaten or processed in a blender until completely smooth before adding remaining ingredients. Otherwise, the finished cheesecake might have a grainy texture.

■ Once the cheese is beaten until smooth and fluffy, add the other ingredients slowly, beating or stirring gently. If you beat too much air into the mixture at this stage, the cheesecake might puff up beautifully during baking, then fall drastically, producing a dense cheesecake with a deeply cracked top.

■ Cheesecakes baked in a very slow oven for a longer period of time will shrink less when cooled.

■ Don't open the oven door during the first 30 minutes of baking time—drafts can cause a cheesecake to fall or crack.

■ To allow for variations in ovens, test a baked cheesecake 5 to 10 minutes before the minimum time indicated in a recipe.

■ Partially cooling a cheesecake in the oven, with the oven door ajar, helps prevent cracks in the top of the cheesecake.

■ Concentric cracking and/or an over-browned top indicate that either the oven heat was too high or the cheesecake was baked too long.

■ Set a baked cheesecake on a rack to cool. After 30 minutes, run a thin-bladed knife between cheesecake and pan to loosen. Continue cooling cheesecake until it reaches room temperature.

■ Leave a cooled cheesecake in its pan, cover tightly, and refrigerate overnight or for at least 6 hours before serving. This allows it to set, makes it easier to cut and makes the texture creamier.

■ Cracks do not ruin a cheesecake! Disguise any scars with a topping such as slightly sweetened sour cream or whipped cream, fresh berries, your favorite jam (stir until easily spreadable or stir in a tablespoon of liqueur). Let any filling sink into the cracks for a few minutes, then add more if necessary so the surface is even.

Chocolate-Chipped Vanilla Scones

These tender, chocolate-studded scones are quick and easy to make and guaranteed to bring on smiles any time of day. Don't think of them as only breakfast or teatime fare—they're also great split and used for berry or peach shortcakes. The most important thing to remember when making quick breads (those made with leavenings other than yeast) is to handle them with care. Overworking the dough will produce a dense, heavy or tough bread. For the flakiest scones, the butter chunks should be about ³⁄₈-inch. And the butter is the only ingredient that should be cold—all others should be at room temperature. In this recipe, warm up refrigerator-cold cream in the microwave oven for 30 seconds.

Makes 8 scones

Chocolate Butter (page 50) or Chocolate-Vanilla Cream (page 108), optional
1³⁄₄ cups all-purpose flour
¹⁄₃ cup confectioners' sugar
2 teaspoons baking powder
¹⁄₂ teaspoon salt
¹⁄₂ cup cold butter, cut into 12 pieces
¹⁄₂ cup semisweet chocolate chips
²⁄₃ cup plus 1 teaspoon whipping cream, room temperature
1 tablespoon plus ¹⁄₄ teaspoon pure vanilla extract
1 teaspoon Vanilla Sugar (page 79) or plain granulated sugar

Prepare Chocolate Butter or Chocolate-Vanilla Cream, if using. Grease a large baking sheet; set aside. Preheat oven to 400°F.

In a large bowl, combine flour, sugar, baking powder and salt. Use a pastry cutter or 2 knives to cut in butter until mixture resembles *very* coarse crumbs. Stir in chocolate chips. Combine ⅔ cup of the cream and 1 tablespoon vanilla; add to flour mixture, stirring only until dry ingredients are moistened. *Or* prepare in a food processor: Place flour, sugar, baking powder and salt in the bowl fitted with the metal chopping blade; process 15 seconds. Add butter and chocolate chips; process in quick ON/OFF pulses only until mixture resembles *very* coarse crumbs (the blade will cut the butter further in the next step). Turn machine off; add liquid mixture. Process in quick ON/OFF pulses only until dry ingredients are moistened. *Do not overprocess.*

Turn dough out onto a generously floured work surface. Gently press dough together and pat into a circle about ¾ inch thick and 7½ inches in diameter. In a small bowl, combine remaining 1 teaspoon cream and ¼ teaspoon vanilla. Brush cream mixture over top of dough; sprinkle with Vanilla Sugar. Use a sharp knife to cut dough circle into 8 wedges. Place wedges, 2 inches apart, on prepared baking sheet. Bake about 15 minutes, or until golden brown. Serve hot with Chocolate Butter or Chocolate-Vanilla Cream, if desired.

Chocolate
and
Vanilla

Chocolate-Vanilla Cream

Excellent on muffins, pancakes, waffles, French toast—you name it.

Makes about ¾ cup

1 (3-ounce) package cream cheese, softened
5 tablespoons butter, softened
1–2 tablespoons confectioners' sugar
1 teaspoon pure vanilla extract
1–3 tablespoons milk
¼ cup grated semisweet chocolate

In a medium bowl, beat cream cheese, butter, sugar and vanilla until smooth. Add enough milk to create a smooth, light spread. Fold in grated chocolate. Cover and refrigerate. Let stand at room temperature 20 to 30 minutes before serving.

■ **Chocolate-Vanilla Butter:** Substitute 5 tablespoons softened butter for the cream cheese, bringing the total amount of butter to 10 tablespoons.

Appendix

Comparative Pan Sizes

There are times when cooks simply don't have the size pan called for in a recipe. The following table will help determine substitutions of pans of similar sizes. For example, if a recipe calls for an 8-inch square baking pan (which has a 6-cup volume), you can see by this table that a 9-inch round cake pan holds approximately the same volume. To measure the volume of a pan or dish, fill it with water, then measure the liquid. The dimensions of a pan are measured from inside edge to inside edge. Measure the depth by standing the ruler in the pan and checking the distance to the rim (don't slant the ruler, as with a pie pan). Remember when making substitutions that baking times will most probably need to be adjusted when pan sizes are changed.

COMMON PAN SIZE	APPROXIMATE VOLUME
1¾" × ¾" mini muffin cup	⅛ cup
2¾" × 1⅛" muffin cup	¼ cup
2¾" × 1⅜" muffin cup	scant ½ cup
3" × 1¼" giant muffin cup	⅝ cup
8" × 1½" pie	4 cups
8" × 1½" round cake	4 cups
9" × 1½" pie	5 cups
8" × 2" round cake	6 cups
9" × 1½" round cake	6 cups
8" × 8" × 1½" square	6 cups
11" × 7" × 2" rectangular	6 cups
7½" × 3" Bundt	6 cups
8½" × 4½" × 2½" loaf	6 cups
9" × 5" × 3" loaf	8 cups

COMMON PAN SIZE	APPROXIMATE VOLUME
9" × 2" pie (deep dish)	8 cups
9" × 2" round cake	8 cups
8" × 8" × 2" square	8 cups
9" × 9" × 1½" square	8 cups
9" × 3" Bundt	9 cups
8" × 3" tube	9 cups
9" × 9" × 2" square	10 cups
9½" × 2½" springform	10 cups
10" × 2" round cake	11 cups
10" × 3½" Bundt	12 cups
9" × 3" tube	12 cups
10" × 2½" springform	12 cups
13" × 9" × 2" rectangular	15 cups
10" × 4" tube	16 cups

High-Altitude Adjustments for Baking

■ Altitudes above 3,500 feet have lower atmospheric pressure, which causes cooked or baked foods to react differently.

■ Foods stored at high altitudes dry out more quickly than those at low altitudes. That means that an ingredient such as flour is drier and will absorb more liquid. Therefore, slightly more liquid or less flour may be required for cake batters or bread and cookie doughs to reach the proper consistency.

■ At high altitudes, leavening must also be adjusted so baked goods don't over-rise; sugar adjustments are necessary to inhibit a porous crumb. These adjustments should be made for baking powder- or baking-soda–leavened bake goods at the following altitudes:

3,000 feet: Reduce leavening by $1/8$ teaspoon for each teaspoon; reduce sugar by $1/2$ to 1 tablespoon per cup; increase liquid by 1 to 2 tablespoons per cup.

5,000 feet: Reduce leavening by $1/8$ to $1/4$ teaspoon for each teaspoon; reduce sugar by $1/2$ to 2 tablespoons per cup; increase liquid by 2 to 4 tablespoons for each cup.

7,000 feet: Reduce leavening by $1/4$ teaspoon for each teaspoon, reduce sugar by 1 to 3 tablespoons for each cup; increase liquid by 3 to 4 tablespoons per cup.

■ For baked goods like cakes, beat egg whites only to soft-peak stage, rather than until stiff.

■ Increase the oven temperature by 25°F for cakes and cookies; slightly decrease baking time.

Index

Index

Index